Be a
Life
Breather

Be a Life Breather

Transform Your Vision into Reality

WORKBOOK

CHELSEA COLLIE

BE A LIFE BREATHER

Copyright © 2020 Chelsea Collie

All rights reserved.

No part of this book may be reproduced, distributed or transmitted in any form by any means, graphic, electronic, or mechanical, including photocopy, recording, taping, or by any information storage or retrieval system, without permission in writing from the publisher, except in the case of reprints in the context of reviews, quotes, or references.

Printed in the United States of America

ISBN: 978-1-64484-090-0

Special discounts are available on bulk quantity purchases by book clubs, associations and special interest groups. For details email: sales@publishyourgift.com or call (888) 949-6228.
For information log on to www.PublishYourGift.com

This book is dedicated to my family, the family I prayed for, for so long.

Thank you to my #1 supporter and loving husband, Sean Collie. You are my rock. Thank you for always being there for me and with me. I'm still head over heels in love with you. I love my life with you. Thank you, sweetheart, for your impeccable patience. Thank you for being so amazing! You make me a better wife, woman, and mother. We are so blessed to have our sweet baby boy. I look forward to raising him together. You truly stole my heart and I love you more and more every day. You are the best man in the whole wide world. Have I told you how amazing you are lately?

A special thank you to Layla, my "Patnah." I love your free spirit, your silly sense of humor, and the fact that you love and forgive so freely. I'm so proud of you. It's amazing to see how much you've grown and risen above. You are absolutely gorgeous. You are a leader, own it. You have so much to offer this world. I'm so grateful we can communicate and rely on each other. Thank you for your support. You truly bring so much joy to my life. I love you so much, sweetheart.

Tyler, I'm so happy you're back. I always want the best for you. I'm proud of you. You are such a hard worker. I know you will be a successful young man. I miss the old days when we had so much fun. I miss being goofy with you and cooking together. I know there are more silly times for us in the future. Always remember family is the most important thing. Best wishes as you venture off to college; you're going to do great. I can't wait to see what you accomplish. I am always here for you. I love you more than you know.

Jaxon, sweet boy, welcome to the world. I love you so much. Your sweet smile melts my heart daily. Although you may have had a rough start, you have a bright future. You are "tough as nails" and "strong as a rock," as your doctors said. It's clear that you are a fighter. You inspire me, and your story has already been an inspiration to many others as well. I thank God that you are a happy healthy boy. You are the biggest blessing we could have received. Thank you for being my first-born and opening my eyes to a whole new life full of experiences I had only dreamed of. You have the best daddy in the world and I'm so glad I get to be your mommy.

Last but not least, Pam. It's scary to think about where I would be without your unconditional love and never-ending support. My mom is so thankful that her best friend kept her promise and you have looked after me my whole life. I could never repay you for all you have done to help, support, and encourage me. I only hope that I can bless you as much as you have blessed me. I love you. Thank you for always telling me to "keep moving forward." That's what it's all about.

Thank you God for blessing me so much in my life! Thank you for all the love. You are loved!

Table of Contents

Foreword ix

Introduction: What Is a Life Breather? 1

Chapter 1: The Power of Choice 5

Chapter 2: The Power of Love 17

Chapter 3: The Power of Self-Love 28

Chapter 4: The Power of Purpose 48

Chapter 5: The Power of Self-Awareness 54

Chapter 6: The Power of Vision 68

Chapter 7: The Power of Strategy 78

Chapter 8: The Power of Execution 83

Conclusion 95

Resources You Can Tap Into 97

About the Author 105

Foreword

Your existence is evidence of your greatness. You arrived on earth having won a race, eager to experience this life and become all you were meant to be. You have infinite potential and as you remember, realize, and embrace this truth, you are equipped with every tool and insight to achieve it.

You have latent qualities, abilities, virtues, gifts, and strengths that are waiting for you to muster the courage, take charge, and start developing them. As you embark on a journey to achieve your highest potential, you will find joy, love, and purpose, and become a blessing to everyone around you.

There may be voices in your head or in your life telling you that you are not capable, lovable, or worthy. You may find yourself as the protagonist of a story that brings you guilt, shame, and suffering. You may only see darkness around you, but your light is seeking to emerge and that's why you found yourself here.

I believe you attract what you are and that's why you're here. You are a life breather and you are yearning to achieve your highest potential. You are ready to be mentored into an experience of positive growth and you are in the right place.

Chelsea Collie introduced herself to me at an event after I shared a vulnerable story as a featured speaker. I knew at first glance that I had found a soul sister. As we began to learn about each other, we discovered that we both had to overcome self-limiting beliefs and self-defeating behavior, and sift through pain to find self-love. I worked with her to give form to this valuable manuscript so you can have the tools to tap into your power and do what we did.

The stories and resources she shares were handpicked to ensure that you succeed in becoming more, doing more, having more, achieving more, and giving more. She pours her heart in the most authentic way to illustrate that you have what it takes to transform your life, and guides you with simple steps you can take to get started.

You are more than your conditions, your circumstances, and the reality of your current life. There are questions throughout this book that will help you focus within and discover who you truly are and who you are meant to be.

I grew up in a slum in extreme poverty, experiencing extreme abuse. But even as a little girl, I decided that I would rewrite my story. I have faced unspeakable tragedies, survived a coma and cancer, and experienced more heartbreak, betrayal, and trauma than I thought I could bear. However, clinging to the truth of my divine nature helped me understand that pain has often led me to my best life, to my best self, to my most beautiful experiences. As you read the pages in this book, you will, like I did, feel a strong connection with the author and feel her genuine love for you. As she shares her own pains and joys, allow yourself to be coachable and teachable. Take the time to dig deep. Uncover the stories that are holding you back and unlock the potential that will "set your life on fire," like ancient poet Rumi encouraged us to do.

Like many others, we have used these universal principles to create a life we love living, to see our dreams manifested, and to lead others as they navigate the path toward expansion. We are here to "fan your flames!"

You are powerful beyond measure and you came here for a purpose, on purpose, with a purpose. May you continue to progress so you can fulfill your glorious destiny, because *progress is success*.

BE Positive and You'll BE Powerful!

Elayna Fernández
The Positive MOM

INTRODUCTION

What Is a Life Breather?

What is a life breather? Depends on who you ask. For some people, it is the person who can light up a whole room. For some, it is a friend providing a shoulder to cry on. For others, it is a mother pouring life into her children and working her tail off in order to put food on the table. For someone that is hurting, a life breather is a person who makes a kind gesture. To me, a life breather is someone who spreads love and speaks life into others. Someone that is a "breath of fresh air" by being kind and welcoming. Someone who bares their soul and breathes life into others by sharing some of the lessons they have learned.

A life breather pours energy into others in the form of love. A life breather is someone who can harness their own personal energy. It is someone who brings the energy up, the second they walk in. Someone who can take an awkward situation and lighten the mood. A life breather can physically transform the energy in a room, making everyone more comfortable around them. It's a person with the brave vulnerability to truly open up and allow others in. A life breather exposes their self-doubts and fears in order to give others the courage to see their own.

We can all become life breathers when we begin to show more love, and we can show more love through our words and actions. We can show more love by being present, simply showing up, and being positive, compassionate individuals.

Not only can we be a "breath of fresh air," we can also achieve our goals and dreams in the process. This book will lay out simple tactics for you to break through the barriers and keep trudging forward no matter what. This book will require you to be honest with yourself about where you are, where you want to go, and where you have been. That information will help you move forward and take action in the most dutiful and fruitful way. The only way is forward.

Here in America, a lot of us are living "stuck," also known as complacent. It appears many of us are "going through the motions," doing what's necessary but not necessarily fulfilling the dreams inside of us. There is pressure to get a good education, a good job, and to make a good living, however, there is not much emphasis on happiness, quality of life, and achieving our dreams. There are expectations coming from all angles—our family, our profession, our children, spouses, and friends—that push us to meet the standards that others have placed on us. But is it what we want?

Do you ever say or hear expressions like "I'm doing ok," "I'm fine," or "Same ole, same ole"? Perhaps you have hesitated to take actions in certain circumstances thinking, "There is nothing I can do about it." Or "This is just the way it is." Or what about the go-to, "I can't afford it."
Many of us are accepting life at face value. But life is not face value. Life is the potential of what can be. The truth is that we are not stuck, we are just seemingly staring at a wall. Only, it isn't a wall, it is a door. We must simply open the door to move forward. Honesty, vulnerability, and courage go hand in hand with moving forward.

> **In the words of the great *Alexander Graham Bell*, "When one door closes, another opens; but we often look so long and so regretfully upon the closed door that we do not see the one that has opened for us."**

The problem is that we are in the problem. But thankfully for us, the solution and the healing are on the other side of that closed door. The solution is far bigger and better than we could ever imagine. Although it sometimes seems impossible, it truly is possible for the universe to deliver exactly what you want, straight into your lap.

We are powerful beyond belief, but when we limit ourselves, everyone loses. We let the fears creep in. We let others get into our head. We lack the confidence we need to take the actions necessary to become who we are meant to be.

Fortunately for you, in this book I have outlined simple strategies to help you elevate yourself to the next level. This book is about YOU! My vision and my intention is to provide tools and opportunities for you to start taking action on those big dreams in your heart.

Take your time with it. Take some time with yourself. Complete the exercises to the best of your ability. You deserve your own care and compassion. Allow yourself to put "you" first. You deserve love, but more importantly, you deserve self-love. You are worth showing up for. Love yourself; you are incredible!

Most people want more love in the world. If we all start loving more, right here, right now, in our own lives, we will elevate ourselves and those around us. You have the power of worlds inside you. Yes worlds, plural! Imagine what you can do for those around you; imagine what you can do for others. Imagine what we can all do together. There truly are no limits. I believe that more love will make the world a better place.

I have made the mistakes. I have learned the lessons. I have paid the price. I was stuck for a long time. Now, I am moving forward full steam ahead. The universe is opening doors I didn't know were there. I know it's all for a divine reason. I can't wait to see what comes to fruition.

I can't wait to see what we can do together. It is time to share my story, my outlook and the methodology that took me from stuck to unstoppable.

MY COMMITMENT TO YOU

My personal commitment to you is to be extremely honest and transparent. My promise to you is to go deep. I will share my experience with loss and grieving, fear of abandonment, and mental illness. I promise to be vulnerable, honest, real and raw. I promise to tell the truth. I promise to talk about the struggles that made me who I am today. I have to tell my truth in order to encourage others to do the same. My promise to you is to say things that others don't and do things that others won't.

The purpose of this book is to give you the tools you need to elevate yourself. When you become a better version of yourself, you can help people in ways that you couldn't before. The best way to elevate yourself and others is through love, the most powerful form of energy.

ABOUT THIS BOOK

In chapters 1–3 you will find my story as well as some of the main concepts, such as, the power of love and the law of attraction. Chapters 4–8 are more of a workbook style where you will define your purpose, learn how to rise above any circumstance, expand upon your vision and start recording your goals. This book is a tool to look at the big picture of your life and your destiny; and arrange your immediate future so that you are constantly progressing towards your greatest goals and dreams.

Your best self and highest potential are waiting. The person you were meant to be wants you to follow your heart and follow your passion. You must breakthrough to your best self. The world needs your gifts.

A life breather speaks the truth. The truth will set us free.

Join me as a life breather and may we never be the same.

CHAPTER 1

The Power of Choice

We have ultimate power within us. Our power is only one choice away.

In every situation, we always have a choice. Sometimes we choose things we want in life and sometimes life chooses for us, but we always have a choice as to how we will react. We don't have to feel powerless. My motto in life is, "10 percent of life is what happens to you and 90 percent is how you react to it." You choose by your actions and your attitude. You don't have to accept every circumstance. You have the power to choose to rise above a situation rather than be victim to it. You don't have to let your setbacks define you. We all have setbacks but it's where we go from there that matters.

Let's choose something great for our lives. Let us live our lives by design and design it well! We can change for the better. It is truly possible, if we are willing. Let us leave what is in the past, in the past. Let us not worry about our future. We must have faith that good things are coming. We must rise and step into our greatest selves, our highest potential. When it comes to our wildest dreams, we can have them. You can have your dream. You can become whoever you want to be. It will be worth it. Let's go for our dreams.

Google's definition of **choice** is "an act of selecting or making a decision when faced with two or more possibilities."

Consider what the power of a choice could do to make your life better. If you knew that you would achieve your wildest dreams and beyond, and all you had to do to begin was to make a choice and believe in it, would you? Your best potential is at your fingertips. You have the power to make your dreams a reality.

Before diving in I would like to share with you some of the experiences that shaped me as a young girl and put me in a situation I could not have foreseen.

MY ROOTS

To help you understand where I am now and where I'm going, I must explain my roots.

I was born in Kansas, the center of the U.S. I grew up with my mom and had a pretty pleasant childhood. We laughed a lot. It was just my mom and I most of the time. We were always doing something fun whether it was festivals, concerts, or fun with family or friends.

She was a nurse. After her long shifts we were able to spend several of her days off together. She was a hardworking single mom and I was an only child. I always wanted a sibling, but it just wasn't in the cards. My mom and I were pretty much best friends. We traveled to California, Vegas, Arkansas, Missouri (Silver Dollar City #best), Colorado and New Mexico, among other places. We loved to go snow skiing which was always fun.

My mom, Dana, came from a big family, the second oldest of six. She grew up on the family farm with her father Wayne, mother Deloris, her siblings, and lots of farm animals including chickens, ducks, geese, rabbits, and her horse, Sam. She loved climbing the tree next to the old barn and getting lost inside a book, sometimes until dark. Her siblings were four boys and one sister, Lana, who she loved dearly.

As for my mom's siblings, Mike was first. Mike is my metal-music-loving-biker-uncle with long hair. I remember him blaring Insane Clown Posse on our vacations. He's hardcore and he's a loving father to his four children, now adults. Just don't piss him off and everything will be good. My mom was born second. Then came my loving Aunt Lana who is the glue that still holds the family together. Then my uncle Dennis who lives in Austin. Then came Jack, who was the fifth child. He still owns the family farm and it's still full of animals. Last was George, the youngest sibling, but more like my mom's little boy; she adored him.

Be a Life Breather

My mom, George and I were always very close. In 2013, while at Lake Wilson, he was trying to help someone, but he didn't put on a life jacket and he drowned. I know he is up there as one of my angels, rooting for and looking out for me.

We were blessed to have a pretty close family when I was growing up. I had a lot of fun playing games with my cousins. All of my family lived two hours away and we were always visiting my mom's family, and my dad's family too. I would visit my dad on occasion. I saw him periodically at my grandparents' house and on holidays. I remember staying with him sometimes and staying up late talking about life and faith.

Growing up, my dad's two sisters, Kathye and Kary were always my fun aunts. They doted on me and I ate it up. We were always getting into trouble running around the small town of Claflin. We frequented the pool, the park, and spent lots of time around horses and rodeos. I even went to their high school with them a couple times! I thought I was just the coolest kid because Kathye, Kary, Grandma Marylin, and Pop Pop had a way of making me feel like the most important person in the world. They had the unique skill of making people feel very special. It was their gift. My Pop Pop, in his overalls was a kick-butt truck driver. He didn't take crap, but he adored me. And my Grandma Marylin was the local "movie star" because she was so beautiful. We had lots of wonderful times.

When I was 10 years old, my dad met Melissa. I'm so grateful for Melissa; she is the best woman on this earth to be his wife. My dad and Melissa got married shortly after meeting each other. Melissa is a very patient woman. She is and always has been an amazing stepmom. All spouses must be profoundly patient. I have learned a lot from Melissa, including how to be a stepmom and how to handle certain situations. She is wise and our family is majorly blessed by her. I have two sisters, Meredith and Cierra from my dad, and they are mommies of beautiful girls.

My Mom and I moved to Austin after elementary school. I was 11 when we moved, just before starting sixth grade. We loved Austin. Living on Lamar, we were right near The Broken Spoke, a famous music venue and bar, and a plethora of restaurants, shops, and theatres. Austin has so much charm. I loved growing up there during middle and high school.

My mom ended up meeting and falling in love with John "Chris" Houston. Chris was the "King of Club Nelray." He was a highly intelligent and wonderful man who was super gifted. He was the ultimate connector and he united everyone. Earlier on, he'd had multiple houses (at different times), all on the same street called Nelray. People started calling it "Club Nelray" because there were always people coming and going. He had an open-door policy and never locked his door. He wanted his house to always be available if someone needed a place to crash. It was a revolving door, the venue for countless parties, concerts, and Sunday potlucks. It was always the "same party, different porch." Chris even began to get mail for Club Nelray, and it just stuck.

The whole Nelray crew welcomed my mom and I and we spent those glory days with so many wonderful and talented people—families, artists, and professionals—basically all hippies and all amazingly fabulous. From the ages of 12 to 16, I had experiences of a lifetime, like canoeing and camping on the Arkansas River. I couldn't go to everything; I was young after all. But they knew how to party. This group of people was incredible and unique. Even though I knew this, I was often "too cool" for any of it. I got bored at the big parties and I was like, "Mom, let's go!" I didn't know our time would be cut short.

June 11, 2000, was a beautiful Sunday morning. I was 16. I got up, talked to my mom, and she French-braided my hair. She wanted to hang out before she had to leave, but I had to go to work at my hostess job at a local chain restaurant. I kissed her goodbye and off I went in my Geo Metro. As I was working, I had a thought while putting a pie in the pie case. What if I never saw my mom again? I stopped after having this thought and my heart started beating fast. My eyes began to water. I was frozen in front of the pie case. It was a sad feeling and it was odd, but I told myself I was being ridiculous. I had these kinds of scary thoughts often, but I told myself to calm down and that I was just being silly. "She's fine," I thought before calling her cell phone.

Be a Life Breather

Mom, Chris, and their three best friends were driving to Dallas to a Roger Waters concert. She didn't pick up when I called, but I heard back from her, saying they'd had a minor hiccup, a flat tire, and had to stop to get a new one. They were back on the highway, she said, headed north towards Dallas. We said "I love you," and that was that. I was glad she was okay.

A little while later, I got a page. At the time, cell phones hadn't been out very long, and I didn't have one, but I had a pager. The number that paged was one I didn't know. But I had gone to a party the night before and gave a guy my pager number. If it was him, I thought, I had to play it cool and not call right away, so I ignored it. But a few minutes later, I got another page, 911. We said 911 all the time, so it didn't necessarily cause concern, but I called anyway.

My mom's friend Carrie was on the other end. She said there had been an accident. She did not know any specifics other than there had been a car accident and we needed to go to the hospital. She instructed me to pack a bag and said she would pick me up. I went home, packed, and called my dad. I told him there had been an accident. "I know," he said. "We are packing and we are going to be on our way very soon." That was alarming. Then he said, "Chris died."
"Chris died?" I replied. My dad confirmed what I thought I heard. He said, "Yes, Chris died at the scene and your mom was life-flighted to Brackenridge hospital." Panic set in. Chris died? No, I thought. If Chris died, did that mean my mom would die? What about Steve, Anne, and Alan, who were also in the car? I was trying to keep calm since I did not yet know the severity, but at this point, the tears came streaming down. I was terrified. I just wanted to know if my mom was okay.

Carrie picked me up and we went to Brackenridge. I had no idea what to expect. We sat in a waiting room full of people, none of whom I knew. A couple minutes later, one of Mom and Chris's friends told me my mom was not going to make it. I started crying. I was so confused. It was a very abrupt statement and I still believe that, among many other things, it could have been handled better. It was the worst feeling ever. A small group of us went into a room and a doctor spoke some gibberish. Cranial something, I heard, but I had no idea what the guy was saying. I wasn't comprehending at all.

I found out that Steve and Anne had some injuries, but were going to be okay. Alan was going to be okay physically, other than scrapes and scratches. They had been treated at a hospital close by the accident and released. They were going to live, but they would have to do it with the memory of that terrible day.

We went up to see my mom in her hospital room. She lay there unconscious, kept alive by the ventilator and all the machines. She was angelic, pale, and bruised. She had two black eyes and stitches above one, but she looked like she was sleeping. I could tell she was my mom, but she didn't look like my mom. The sound of the breathing machine was loud. I could see her chest rising and falling as the machine pumped air in and out of her. I remember this moment vividly. It was surreal. Although it was a real-life moment, it seemed like a dream state because I had never imagined seeing something like that before.

Shortly after, a nun came in. She prayed with me over my mom, then told me that my mom had a 50/50 chance to live. She said if I just prayed, prayed harder than I ever had before, maybe she would have a chance to live. That gave me hope. So I did. I prayed as hard as I could that whole night and into the next day. I laid next to my mom and slept with her in the hospital bed. I spent all night with her. I was holding the small Christmas portrait we had taken together the previous Christmas. Inside my mind, I talked to my mom. I confessed some things I never told her. I apologized for some things and for being a brat. I really felt like I communicated with her, because I did. We had full conversations, no physical words, only the dialogue inside my head. She told me she was proud of me. I told her I needed her. I told her that she was strong and that I couldn't live without her. She said that I could because I was even stronger. I didn't believe it at all.

I tried to bargain with God, telling Him that if He just let my mom live, I would do whatever He wanted for the rest of my life. I felt powerless and helpless. This was way too unbelievable. I kept asking myself, is this really happening?

My family from Kansas arrived the next day and people came and visited her room in the ICU. The waiting room was packed with my family, my mom's friends and my cousins. For whatever reason, I was still unaware of her condition and I didn't know whether or not she still had a fighting chance.

Later that afteroon, my grandma Deloris and I were called into a hospital office; we were her next of kin. There were two other people there who told us they were from the transplant team. They were walking us through some documents and said my mom had elected to be a donor. They asked about her heart, explaining it could give someone else more years. We agreed, and they began going through the list of her other organs, one by one, asking which ones could be donated. I was confused. She was still alive.

"Wait, I'm confused," I said. "Is this just in case she doesn't make it? Why are you asking us this?" The lady responded, "No honey. Didn't anyone tell you? They completed testing this morning. It was confirmed she had no brain activity. She was declared dead at 9 a.m. this morning." That was it. That was the moment I found out my mom was dead. She was just down the hall and still technically alive. However, no one had told me she had been declared dead that morning. My heart sank. The lady went on to explain that the doctors were just keeping her alive to complete the surgeries needed for organ donations.

The confusion, the anger, the frustration rose and I was in total disbelief that my mom's life was over. I wondered how this could have happened. Although they could see my distress, they gave me no time to process. They said we still had to finish the meeting and go through everything. They continued. I wanted to scream. We said yes to donating all of her organs, but opted to keep her eyes. They asked about her skin. This part, beyond others, was really unbelievable to me. After hanging out all day with my family by her side, finding out like this, then hearing these people ask if they could take my mom's skin, I said, "I don't think so." They went on to explain how taking some skin from her stomach and legs could help repair victims who had been severely burned. I said, "Fine." And that concluded the meeting.

I couldn't believe that no one had told me. There I was still hanging on to every bit of hope, praying harder than I ever had before, only to find out in a transplant meeting that my mom was brain dead and would never come back. I felt so alone. Up until that point, I'd had one person I could count on no matter what. I had one person who was like my whole family, my whole support, my whole life. I had one person who looked after me and kept me safe. And she was gone. There were people all around, yet I felt completely alone.

They kept my mom alive to complete the transplant surgeries. In the end, she saved seven people by donating her organs. Her heart went to a dying 86-year-old woman. A young 38-year-old heart gave the woman many more years to enjoy life and spend time with her grandchildren.

A CHOICE

I had a choice. I don't think anyone would have blamed me if I pulled the covers over my head and just shut off life. I could have just given up because I was basically an only child with no mom. Or I could just go on. I could choose to live my life. I could do all the things I had envisioned. I could do all the things I was planning, like college, career, and family. At times, I did want to lay in bed and give up, but I would remember how my mom lived life to the fullest. She didn't take her life for granted and I knew I shouldn't either.

There was only one right choice, and that was to live life every day to the fullest, just as she had. I learned from her that I must not take life for granted. When some people go through hardships they say, "I didn't have a choice." But the truth is that they did. One choice was giving up and giving in, and the other choice was to use that experience as a lesson to keep going. For me, there was only one good option. I had to carry on. No matter what happened, I had to keep moving forward. So I did. I kept going. I kept trudging forward. I cried when I needed to. I leaned on the support of my close high school friends.

> **In the words of *Winston Churchill*,**
> **"If you're going through hell, keep going."**

I thought my life was going to be a certain way. I thought I would continue to grow up with my mom. I thought we had many more experiences together, picking out a college and a wedding dress, but that was not the case. I suffered a great loss, but I gained as well. I felt stronger through this life experience. I felt that if I could get through losing my mom (and stepdad), I could do anything. I allowed myself to dream bigger. I told myself, "If I have to live without my mom, then I'm not going to live a mediocre life."

WHO COULD YOU BECOME IN THE PROCESS OF ACHIEVING MANY OF YOUR WILDEST DREAMS?

Many of us are seeking more passion, more inspiration, more significance from our lives. We have the option now to stay the same or take action on the desires in our heart.

Media mogul Oprah Winfrey never dreamed that she would impact the world in such a big way. The magnitude of all she has been able to give and the people she has been able to serve is truly inspiring. She prayed when she was a little child for God to use her. And he did! She has moved mountains and had an impact on millions of people! She has shared personal stories of abuse and growing up in poverty and become a trustworthy source, in part, because of that vulnerability. She considers her audience when interviewing others. She has the great ability to ask direct questions that her audience wants to know.

Let us go big like Oprah and trudge forward to "Step up into our greatness." Let's step boldly and courageously into the person we want to be. We must recognize we have power in every situation. We always have a choice. We can choose to let hardships define us or not. We can choose to accept certain relationships or not. We can choose to accept something, change it, or let it go.

No matter what decision you make, it is important to remember that you are #1, and it's up to you to save yourself. No one is coming to your rescue. And it wouldn't be permanent anyway if they did. You must come to your own rescue. You must be your own hero.

Ask yourself the following questions and consider your answers.

- Is it possible to achieve my dreams?
- Am I allowing someone or a situation to limit my potential?
- Am I holding myself back? If yes, how?
- Do I believe I have the power to choose my destiny?
- Can I overcome my limitations to move forward with tenacity?

> **In the words of the great leader and author *John Maxwell*, "Life is a matter of choices, and every choice you make makes you."**

The Power of Choice Exercise

This exercise will illustrate the power of choice in your life. Complete this exercise and let's keep moving forward.

Think of a time when you experienced a life-changing event. Think of two choices you could have made after the event or two options you had at the time.

What were your two choices?

_____

_____

Which choice did you make? Why?

_____

_____

Looking back, do you feel like you made the right choice? Why or why not?

_____

_____

What lesson did you learn, having had this experience?

_____

_____

REFLECTION QUESTION

Is there something that has been weighing heavily on your heart that you need to make a decision about? What choice could you make that might help the situation?

_____
_____
_____
_____
_____
_____
_____
_____
_____
_____
_____
_____
_____
_____
_____
_____

CHAPTER 2

The Power of Love

Love is the most powerful tool and strength we possess.

What is the power of love? How does that work exactly? The answer is that it's all energy. Science shows us that the building block of all matter is energy. Everything is made of energy. I believe the highest and most powerful form of energy is love.

Being a life breather is about elevating yourself by honoring your dreams and passions. During this process the positive energy you generate pours outward. That good energy is, essentially, love. Being a life breather is about spreading love and becoming better so we can help others become better. That process happens through love.

LOVE IS IN YOUR HEART

Every bit of life started in our hearts. When we were a tiny seed in our mother's womb, our lives began with one spark, our first heartbeat. The brain came after. This order of events was no coincidence. I believe the brain came after because our hearts are our main source of power and strength throughout our lives. Our hearts possess the physical strength we need to master great feats as well as the inner strength to do that which we aspire to do. We find the power of love in our hearts.

Love begets love. Love produces more love. Love has infinite power. Love is our power. Love is our superpower. Love is a feeling within us.

When I was a child, I was confused when people said, "I love you with all my heart." I heard one person say it to more than one person. I asked myself, how can they love different people with "all of their heart?" I remember being at my Grandma's house when the question came to me, and when my mom picked me up, I asked her on the car ride home how this was possible. "If we love so many people so much," I said, "how come our love doesn't run out?" She thought for a second and responded, "Love can never run out because love creates more love." She went on to describe how love is infinite. Once you love someone, it keeps growing and growing, forever.

When you have love in your heart and the mind is connected, it's real. It's all energy. I'll prove it to you so that you can start the process to achieving all your dreams, your true potential, and your desired future self.

You can literally feel the power of love in any moment. There is power in your heart.

The Power of Your Heart Exercise

After reading this section, try closing your eyes and putting your hands on your chest, over your heart. Feel the power of your heartbeat. Feel for the sensation deep inside your chest and at the bottom of your throat. Then, with your eyes still closed, take a second to breathe deeply and just love. Focus on the love. Breathe into the love. When you concentrate, you can feel the love grow. Be silent. Be focused. Tune in.

Go ahead and take a few minutes to go through that process of feeling the love, and come back after you have felt it.

As long as you're focused, you can physically feel love growing with every heartbeat. You can feel it all over your entire body, from your fingers to your toes. Let that love fill you up and envelop you. Picture in your mind a shield that surrounds your entire body. The love that surrounds you will elevate you, protect you and hold you in a good, intentional place.

If you did this every day, do you think it would make a difference and elevate you? Absolutely. This love energy is actually more real than the cup of water I'm currently drinking, more real than the book you are holding in your hand. Love is the most powerful form of all energy. To further explain why I believe this, I must introduce two books, *The Secret* and *The Power*, and a concept called the law of attraction. I highly recommend these two books written by Rhonda Byrne. I also recommend the movie of the same name, *The Secret,* which is a powerful series of interviews, released in 2006.

THE SECRET

Being a student of personal development early on, I was introduced to the book, *The Secret*. When Rhonda Byrne released the book in 2005, many people wondering, "Well what is the secret?!" If you have not read the book or seen the movie, forgive me for spoiling it for you, but "the secret" is the law of attraction.

LAW OF ATTRACTION

The law of attraction states that like energy attracts like energy. The law suggests that thoughts become things and that you can manifest outcomes and objects in your life through your thoughts and beliefs.

Urban dictionary provides this summary: "The Law of Attraction is a New Age belief based on the concept that "like attracts like" and that by focusing on positive thoughts, such as affirming to yourself that you will win a million dollars, your thoughts and affirmations will subsequently manifest themselves by granting you the one million dollars. Your thoughts are similar to magnets. Positive thoughts will attract positive outcomes and vice versa for negative thoughts."

Here is a quote referenced in *The Secret*:

> "Whatever the mind can conceive it can achieve."
> —*W. Clement Stone*

It is real. If you want it to be. It is real that you can manifest things in your life. I have experienced it in my life.

HOW I KNOW IT WORKS

In 2017, I created a vision board. On it I put several things I loved and wanted, places I wanted to go and things I wanted to achieve. One of the achievements I desired most was to be a mother. I have had the honor and privilege of being a mom to two wonderful step kids for years, but I still wanted to have at least one of my own. On my vision board I put a big pregnant belly and a positive pregnancy test. I set my intention in 2017 that by the end of 2018 I would be expecting a child.

Despite the fact that I had been trying to conceive for a couple years and had about 100 negative pregnancy tests, after placing those images on my vision board I became pregnant in August of 2018. I was in shock. I just stared at the positive test. I knew my stomach had been a little queasy, but I thought I couldn't get pregnant, so I did not allow my mind to believe I could be until I saw the positive test result. A short time later, while sitting in my office, I told my husband Sean the great news. He looked up at the wall above my desk and said, "It's coming true." There above me, on my vision board, was the pregnant belly and positive pregnancy test.

That moment was magical. Tears come to my eyes even now when I think about it. To know that my prayers and wishes were answered despite my hesitations and my questioning whether or not I was even ready for a baby, was complete confirmation. The universe took my order and it delivered. The test even looked the same as the one on my vision board, except instead of two pink lines, it had two blue lines. And wouldn't you know, it was a boy.

These kinds of things happen all the time. They can happen to you. You simply must believe. If you can believe you can have it, it will be yours. It's the way energy works in our world. Your greatest dreams are an ask and a belief away. Don't underestimate the law of attraction.

You can start using the law of attraction now to attract what you want in life. Use this power to call on your dreams, to begin to achieve your highest potential.

Now that you know what the law of attraction is, here is how you can implement it in your life. You simply follow the three steps laid out in the *The Secret*.

> ## 3 STEPS TO THE LAW OF ATTRACTION:
>
> 1. <u>ASK</u> for what you want.
> 2. <u>BELIEVE</u> with sincerity that you already have what you want.
> 3. <u>RECEIVE</u> it and be grateful that your request was granted.

My takeaway from *The Secret* was that if you can see it and believe it, then you can have it. The universe will deliver it to you. I think many people like me have always felt that momentum but could never find a way to name it or talk about it. The law of attraction can help you achieve and obtain anything you want.

A VALUABLE TIP:

You can access the movie *The Secret* on Netflix. If you really want to accelerate your momentum, watch it three nights in a row. It is powerful. I don't know why it's so powerful, but by doing this, I was able to get out of a rut and start moving forward again with a renewed mindset.

THE POWER

A while back I read the sequel to *The Secret*, Rhonda Byrne's book *The Power*. If you enjoy learning about the law of attraction and are intrigued by what the power of love could do in your life, you absolutely must read it. I found that *The Power* simply defines the law of attraction and truly opens your mind to what is possible through more love in your life.

A VALUABLE TIP:

If you use the app Audible, these two book recordings, *The Secret* and *The Power*, are an exciting listen! Play it while you sleep to access your subconscious mind.

Assuming you have not read *The Power*, the power named in the book is love. Rhonda Byrne goes on to explain that the law of attraction is a truly powerful force that is, essentially, love. The way the world works is that you move towards things you love, and you move away from things you don't love. That energy in the law of attraction is love, which is the highest form of energy. Reading that book put a whole new spin on things for me because it helped me to understand the power of love and the potential effect it could have on our lives.

I have always believed in the saying that love conquers all. I have always felt that love is the reason we are here. *The Power* provided more information, proof, and confirmation for what I already knew. I realized that love is the greatest of all things. It is the purpose and the reason we are here on Earth. We are to love above all else. Love is greater than negative energy, gravity, and even greater than positive energy. Love is the greatest energy of all, because true love empowers. I believe every problem and situation can be made better through more love. For example, if you are upset with a friend for saying something hurtful, consider that something in their past experience has made them feel this way. Decide not to take it personally and forgive them for the hurt it caused you.

This is good news people! We can change our whole lives with more love! If we can ask, believe, and affirm ourselves in the mirror with love, we will receive what we ask for. We can become anyone we want. If we believe it, the universe must deliver it. Now let us open up our minds and start dreaming again, even bigger! Let us not sell ourselves short. Who says we can't if we say we can?

Use love to forgive yourself. Love yourself enough to believe you deserve to receive the big dreams in your heart. And start! Rise up and say you can. Do t for the reason of more love! Call it what you want, but when you truly open up your heart to the world, the whole world will open up to you. Believe it; it is the truth!

Why are we not using love to obtain anything and everything we want?! This is the question I asked myself after reading and understanding *The Power*. The answer to that question is why I wrote this book! People need to know they have the power within them, and they need to know that the power is love. We can use love as the most effective tool to get along with our families, further our careers, and pursue our wildest dreams.

HOW DO LIFE BREATHERS SHOW MORE LOVE?

The easiest way to implement more love in our lives is to start with our own words. Life breathers help others by sharing healing words, words that people desperately want and need. With words, we can not only become a better version of ourselves, we can improve our relationships. We are human creatures who need to coexist with other humans. We need each other. We are meant to lean on one another. We need to speak life into others with our words. We need our words to lift others up, not bring them down. We need to feel heard, loved, and accepted.

Everyone needs others to show compassion for them. As we all know, life is too short not to say the words like, "I love you," "I'm sorry," and "I appreciate you." Or, "I didn't mean to hurt you." With our words, we show love, and with more love, everyone is elevated. If we all started loving more in our lives, there would be less sadness, more fulfillment, and more connection in the world.

It is important to go to your family and loved ones directly and share the unspoken words that show your love for them. Tell them the things they want to hear. Tell them the things they need to hear. Say the things they never thought they would hear. Make them feel special, valued, and loved by you whenever possible. Tell them you love them, that you see them doing their absolute best, and that you admire that about them. Whatever it is you feel, and have never said, say that. Life is too short not to say what you truly feel.

Show your love in the form of hugs, smiles, happiness, excitement, jumping up and down and more hugs! Take the time to get all the love in. Take time while you can because they can easily be gone and, eventually, they will be gone and it will be too late.

Thumper, in the movie *Bambi* said, "If you can't say something nice, don't say nothing at all." However, somewhere along the line, that got mixed up and people mistakenly got the impression that when they're not sure what to say, it's best to not say anything. Although this may be acceptable under some circumstances, like a big-time business meeting, it's not the way it's always supposed to be. Not at home anyway. When it comes to your loved ones, it is best to say too much rather than not enough.

Try giving someone a compliment. For example, "Hey I just wanted to say what a pleasure it was to have such wonderful service today. You really went above and beyond, and we appreciate that." Pause. Smile. And just give them the gift of having that moment of appreciation. Tip everyone extremely well! Throw them a $20 if they brightened your day. Tipping is important.

What you give you get back, so give well, generously, and often!

Whether it's in the form of words, money, hugs, a shout out, a phone call, a letter, or even a text, give freely!

> **In the words of *Helen Keller*, "The best and most beautiful things in the world cannot be seen or even heard but must be felt with the heart."**

Ask yourself the following questions and consider your answers.

- What if there was more love in the world?
- What happens when we spread love like mad and pour life into others with our words?
- What would happen if I started speaking kind words and smiled more to the people around me?
- What words do I need to hear to feel more loved?
- What if loving words are the medicine we need most in life?

The Power of Love Exercise

How are you showing love to your loved ones currently?

_____

_____

What actions or practices could you start implementing to show even more love to your loved ones?

_____

_____

Is there someone around you that is yearning for some appreciation? Is there someone who keeps popping up in your mind that you need to reach out to? How can you show up for them and show them you care with your words or your actions?

_____

_____

What is something that you want to accomplish in the future that could help others? How does that accomplishment show love to those you want to help?

_____

_____

REFLECTION QUESTION

How could you add even more love to your everyday life?

CHAPTER 3

The Power of Self-Love

When it comes to love, start with the person in the mirror.

We have all heard it and most know it to be true; we are our own worst critic. We are harder on ourselves than we are on others. Oftentimes, we are quick to forgive others but we hold on to guilt for years. For example, sometimes when I sleep in, I get down on myself. If I mention it to someone else they will point out the fact that I'm a new mom and I probably needed the rest. We often hold ourselves to a higher standard than we do other people. If we began to treat ourselves as we would treat a best friend, we would be able to show ourselves love and love ourselves more.

It is human nature to love, therefore, love for others should come easily. However, our past relationships, experiences, and beliefs can make it difficult. We are constantly sizing ourselves up and analyzing if we are doing well or not. We ask ourselves questions like: Am I doing my best? Am I doing the right thing? Should I be doing something else?

When we were children, we had people who taught us, whether it be our parents or someone else. They taught us right from wrong and taught us how the world works. Whether or not we received accurate information doesn't matter because we grew up believing what we saw and were told. As a result, we have others' voices in our heads—their advice, critiques and criticism. Some of us, like myself, feel like we should be further along in our lives and we should have made more progress. In addition to that, we are constantly comparing ourselves to others, which only makes things worse.

For me, one of my greatest judgments of myself is feeling like I have wasted too much time. I felt that since my mom did not have the luxury of having more time, I should have made the best of mine. That judgement ties back to my own personal painful experience. I show love to myself by forgiving myself for time wasted. I have given myself grace and come to terms with the fact that it's hard enough to lose a parent and best friend, I didn't need to add guilt on top of it.

WHY IS SELF-LOVE IMPORTANT?

Self-love is essential for a full life. If we don't love ourselves, we hold ourselves back. A person that does not love themselves has little confidence, is quick to anger, and slow to forgive. Without self-love we are never truly, "comfortable in our skin." Someone who does not love themselves does not like who they have become. They don't have faith in themselves. They don't have respect for themselves. We must love ourselves because, in the end, other than our higher power, we're all we've got.

There were so many times in my life that I put faith in others who let me down, which led me to be sad and angry. I felt like time and time again, I would learn that I could only depend on myself. When I began to love myself more, people's actions hurt less. Loving myself showed me who I truly am. I know my heart now and I know my intentions were good.

If you can show love to yourself, you can effectively accept love from others. If you are not able to love yourself, you cannot fully accept love from others because you do not deem yourself as "lovable." In order to love outwardly, we must first love inwardly first. True love goes both ways.

Taking it one step further, when it comes to helping others, we must first help ourselves. When on an airplane, you are instructed to out on your own oxygen mask first before helping others, if the oxygen masks come down. Similarly, if you want to show love by helping others, you must love yourself first. We can only give what we have. If our intention is to help others and help them make a difference in their lives, we can only help them to the extent that we have helped ourselves.

Telling my story has been the most difficult part of this whole book-writing process, because self-love has been a challenge for me. But while writing my story has been painful, it has also been very rewarding. If self-love is something you struggle with, I recommend you tell your own story and show yourself love in that process. It is difficult, but it will be worth it.

> **In the words of the beautiful *Brené Brown*, "Loving ourselves through the process of owning our story is the bravest thing we will ever do."**

Telling the next part of my story requires that I reveal some of the difficulties I've had with self-love, but they will help you understand how my life progressed.

MY STORY, CONTINUED

When my mother passed away, I had to become a "grown-up," virtually overnight. There I was, sixteen, raised as an only child by a single mom who suddenly died in a car accident with her fiancé; it was a heavy burden to carry. In the beginning, I was determined to make the best of it to make my mom proud. I was committed to carrying on and not letting her death stop my life. I made a choice to continue. I decided I would keep moving forward, no matter what.

My uncle had moved to Austin a couple of years before and was living with one of my mom's friends. When the accident happened, he told me that he would move back into the house so that I could stay in Austin. The last thing I wanted to do was move to a small town in Kansas with my dad and lose, not only my mother and stepdad, but all my friends and my home as well. I love my dad but in my mind, there was no way I was going to Kansas to live with him. As a sixteen-year-old girl, I was naturally closer to my mom. My dad and I didn't have that close of a relationship. The thought of leaving everything I knew behind made it clear that I would be miserable there, not to mention the culture shock of going from South Austin city life to the cow town of Great Bend, Kansas.

Up to that point, my mom had trusted me. I had pretty much done what I wanted to do. I preferred to go it alone than be under the responsibility and authority of my dad. On top of being raised "leniently," this huge loss gave me full freedom. I wasn't about to give that up.

I continued with everything that I had planned to do. I stayed in high school and on drill team, and continued with my junior and senior year. I continued working as a hostess at a local chain restaurant. Since I was in the house with no parents, I had all the parties. I was the "hostess with the mostest." I loved having people and friends over. I always made sure everybody had a drink and everyone was comfortable. My uncle was there, but there was little to no communication. I was pretty much on my own.

My mother apparently made a will but she, unfortunately, never told us where she put it. We didn't find the will anywhere. There were no instructions regarding it so we had to operate as if there was not one, which put us in probate court. While going through this process, which lasted a while, I would miss school, drive downtown, pay to park, and go into the courthouse where the case was delayed practically every month. Probate court was a horrible, difficult process, especially after experiencing such a huge loss. From the court process and the lawyers, to the life insurance payout, everything was extremely difficult and a heavy burden to carry over the course of the two-plus years that followed. I'm sure if my mom had to do it over again, she would have had a will and filed it properly so that I wouldn't have had to go through it. I am certain, though, that my Mom thought she had more time.

If you are a parent, please get a will! It is an absolute must. You never know when your time is up.

My uncle Dennis came to court and testified that my mom left everything to me. I was named the sole heir of my mom's estate. We proceeded, and I became emancipated, granting me the full rights of an adult. I inherited my mom's house and assets. Being emancipated, I was able to get a car loan and open specific accounts. I even wrote my own sick notes and late notes for school. Everything short of buying cigarettes, I could do at the age of 16. I was on my own and operating as such. It took a whole year for us to receive my mom's life insurance payout and all the while, we were pretty short on money. I received Social Security so that helped. Dennis and I often shared the little Geo Metro I was given on my 16th birthday. We got a lot of use out of that $1,100 car!

With all of the life-altering changes, it was a difficult, complicated time. Junior year was a tough year. Although it was the hardest year of my life up to that point, my friends really kept me going. They became my family. I didn't often break down, but when I did, they were there for me.

I will admit, it was hard to sit around and listen to girls complain about their mothers when mine was gone. I just wanted to tell them, "Appreciate her. Be glad you have her." And sometimes I did. But more often than not, I kept my sad feelings to myself because I didn't want to bring down the energy and turn a good time into a sad time. I knew they didn't know what to say or do, so I didn't want to make the situation uncomfortable. I just kept going. I hadn't experienced feeling the loss and grief yet. I soldiered through. I trudged on. I had a lot of fun in the process. And I made some lifelong friends that I remain close with, to this day.

THE LAWSUITS

You may or may not remember, but in summer of 2000 there was a huge tire recall for Ford Explorer's Firestone tires. There were over 271 fatalities and 800 injuries in the US due to tread separation on Firestone tires used on the Ford Explorer. The majority of the accidents took place in Texas, Arizona, Florida and California. Unfortunately, my mom and Chris were two of the people who perished as a result. The accident happened in June of 2000 and the tires were recalled in August.

The accidents were a combination of things, a "perfect storm;" a series of malfunctions and events. Originally Ford had an excess of frames for the Ford Ranger and they came up with the idea of using the Ford Ranger frame for the Ford Explorer SUV. Instead of designing a frame from scratch, they could solve two problems by designing the Explorer on the Ford Ranger frame. The problem was that the Ford Ranger was a smaller truck, and had a lower center of gravity. Since the center of gravity is higher in an SUV, Ford Explorers were more prone to rollovers.

Ford used the smaller frame and recommended a lower tire pressure, which would help to keep gas consumption down. Therefore, they promoted it as the most "gas-friendly" SUV on the market. Also, Ford designed a lighter roof, and when an overturned vehicle flipped, it would shatter the windshield. Once the car rolled and the windshield shattered, the lighter roof collapsed and caved into the vehicle. The combination of a lower than recommended tire pressure, being prone to rollovers, the smaller frame, the roof collapse and the addition of warm temperatures and high speeds, was the perfect storm for many horrific events.

There was much more to the story, including the factory in Decatur, Illinois with overworked employees that eventually closed, a Firestone cover-up, compounded by Ford standing up for Firestone, and the fact that it was the #1 selling SUV in America at the time, which made them turn a blind eye and be tragically slow to react. Attorneys argued Ford and Firestone knew about the dangers but did nothing about it.

By May of 2000, the month before the accident, the Firestone tires on the Explorers were recalled in multiple countries with warmer climates, but they waited in the US because of sheer profits. I believe if the recall happened in May, my mom and Chris would still be alive today.

Firestone allocated close to one billion dollars for lawsuit settlements and I'm pretty sure they still came out on top, which is disgusting to me. I can't begin to explain how infuriating it is that Ford and Firestone delayed the recall because the Ford Explorer was the best-selling SUV at the time. It's incredibly heartbreaking that a corporation, two corporations, would knowingly risk the lives of their customers for the sake of increasing profits. I cannot understand something like that; it will always baffle me. I have to accept it and keep moving forward.

All that being said, we connected with a great lawyer and proceeded with the process of filing lawsuits against Ford and Firestone. After several months, we made a settlement with Ford and sometime later, we settled with Firestone. It was truly bittersweet. I was glad to have the money, but it also felt terrible to accept that money because Ford and Firestone had essentially put a price on my mom's life. They thought they could take her and pay me later. It is a hard thing to say, but it was blood money. But the way I chose to look at it is that if my mom had a choice about the way she went, she would have wanted to provide for me. So I was thankful that I didn't have to worry about money for a period of time.

During high school, it was a difficult to come to terms with losing my mom, but I did have one constant love, and that was from my Chula. Chula was my mom's dog, who became my daughter when my mom passed. Chula was a little Pomeranian who was adorable and sassy. She was always there for me. I trudged through the rest of high school doing high kicks on the way. I graduated in South Austin in May 2002. I loved having parties so much that I decided to go to school for Hotel Management with an emphasis in Sales and Event Management. I moved to Houston for college and attended the Conrad Hilton School of Hotel Management, and I took my little Chula with me.

COLLEGE YEARS

I got settled in my new apartment and started school in the fall semester. I loved my Hotel Management major and enjoyed my classes. I started making friends. I decided to join a sorority. It was a good group of girls. Soon my calendar was full of social activities and school activities. There were a lot of good times.

Since I inherited my first house when I was 16, real estate investing was not on my mind at the time. However, I did have a passion for real estate and what you could do while investing in it. My godmother Pam stepped in to help me during college. Pam and I have always been very close and she had promised my mom that if anything happened to her, she would look after me. The proceeds from the lawsuits were all in a trust. Because of the way the trust was set up, I would always have a trustee. Pam was very good in finance and she had my best interest at heart, so she took over my trust and helped me with finances. She also helped me make some good decisions with real estate. I'm very blessed to have Pam in my life to this day. I would not have anything if it weren't for her.

Be a Life Breather

Since I no longer needed the house in Austin, I sold it to my uncle. It was hard for me to sell it to him because I knew he wouldn't take care of it. Even though I felt that way, ultimately, I was happy that my uncle would have a house and I was grateful that it could stay within the family. I used that money to purchase my house in Houston. I had two roommates whose rental payments covered the low monthly mortgage, all the bills, and left me with some extra. Owning a home in college and having roommates was a great way to avoid having to pay a monthly rent.

At first glance, it would seem like owning a home and having a trust in my name is a favorable situation, but knowing how I had come upon the money made me feel shameful and guilty. On one hand, I was glad to have the money. On the other hand, I hated having the money because I had to lose my mom to get it. I not only felt ashamed for having it, I felt shame for spending it. People would ask how I could afford a house and how I supported myself. I even got the occasional comment, "Oh your parents must pay for everything." I never knew how to respond to those questions and would change the subject and avoid those conversations altogether. It was too hard to tell the truth of what happened, so I just didn't bring it up or talk about it at all. Any questions about parents and/or money were very hard for me. I would spend more money to relieve the pain, then I would feel even worse.

Looking back, I can see how the law of attraction was working against me. I was in a vicious cycle. I felt guilt and self-judgment when I had money in my account so I would spend it quickly on something I didn't need, which led right back to feelings of guilt and shame. But since I had decided I was not taking life for granted, I said yes to everything. I spared no expense. Any concert I wanted to go to, done. If I wanted to travel, I did. If my friends didn't have money, that was okay because I wanted to go out and I would pay. I know it was uncomfortable for them at times, but then again, if I wanted to do something, they would support me and we would go do it. I was attracting some great life experiences but with those, I was also attracting the guilt that came along with it.

I made a lot of unhealthy decisions with my money, spending frivolously. My experience taught me that life was fleeting, so I tried to have as much fun as I could, while I could. If there was something I wanted, I got it. I would feel bad, spend money, feel better for a short period of time and then feel guilty and spend money again to feel better. Life was a constant rollercoaster.

Throughout college I had various (short-lived) jobs as a cocktail waitress, hostess, event staff and a front desk attendant at a hotel. I was late often, and whenever life seemed to conflict with my jobs, I would quit. For example, if I wanted to go to Kansas for the holidays and my job wouldn't let me off, I would resign. Or I was fired, that happened too.

There was good and bad, but I had fun in college. I don't think I ever missed a party. I met my bestie, Jessica, in my sorority. We were all about the live music scene and took road trips all over Texas, following our favorite bands around.

DEPRESSION

A few years into college, there was a horrible drunk driving accident in which a friend of ours was killed. She was vice president in our sorority. It was a sudden, tragic loss that hit home for our whole sorority and Greek community. After that, my depression kicked in. Her death brought up all kinds of feelings of loss for my friend and my mom. I was feeling the grief I had never faced in high school. I went to a counselor for a short period of time and began taking anti-depressants, which seemed to work well for me in the beginning.

Depression would come in and out, often coinciding with how much I was partying. There were times when I would skip school for a whole week and catch up the next week. I found that much of the sadness I experienced was the result of repressed feelings from the past.

In high school, everyone knew about the loss of my mom. But in college, no one knew unless I told them. I felt like I needed to get to know people before I would confide in them about my mom. I could always just pretend like everything was okay, and that was often the default choice. Keeping these important parts of me to myself, unknowingly, put up a wall between me and everyone else. It sent the message to keep topics surface level. Don't get too close. Although it appeared I was always up for a good time, staying quiet inhibited me from developing more "quality" relationships. I had very few close friends as a result.

This wasn't life breather behavior. I was too scared that people would either judge me or take advantage of me. When I think about self-love, looking back, it makes me sad. I wasn't showing myself love and compassion. I felt embarrassed because I was alone with no family around. It felt shameful to me, like it was something to hide. It made me feel unwanted, abandoned, or like an orphan. If I could go back in time and talk to the younger me, I would tell myself that I was a good daughter. I was a kind and compassionate person and I deserved to be kind and compassionate toward myself. I would have encouraged myself to open up and share my story, share my feelings, share my pain because the relief of expression would ease some of the pain. For the most part, though, I never dealt with the pain of losing my mom. I still had that hollow feeling inside, the feeling of abandonment.

I graduated in December of 2006 after four and a half years. That spring, I moved back to Austin, and over the next few years, many things stayed the same. I was still spending beyond my needs and still in party mode, which began to have more and more of a detrimental effect on my life.

BIPOLAR DIAGNOSIS

I got a decent job working in the sales office of a hotel in downtown Austin and purchased a home in South Austin shortly after. It was beautiful and perfect, in a nice neighborhood. I closed on the house October 29, 2007. On Halloween, the city turned on my water while I was at work. The flap on the upstairs master toilet tank was open. When the water was turned on, it continued to fill up and overflow the toilet tank, and it didn't stop. All day long my upstairs bathroom flooded to the point where almost the entire house was wet and it was raining downstairs in the kitchen. I didn't get home until late in the evening. Chula was home and she was scared and soaking wet. It was a horrible experience and the feeling was defeating. In a matter of two days, my perfect new home had become a flood zone. Fortunately, insurance covered it. The water removal company told me my house would be good as new in two to three months.

While they moved forward with the cleanup, I tried to balance a brand-new job and trying to make a good impression while dealing with contractor calls, coordinating visits, and the insurance claim. It was a tough time for me. I was staying in my house and doing my best to live in a construction zone. Since I couldn't leave work, I had to leave a key on my back porch for the contractors to let themselves in and out. Any given day, a number of people were in and out of my house, but I didn't know who, how many, or when. When I would get home, I didn't know if there were any workers still there in the house or not.

There was an attic door in my master closet and every day when I came home, I would double check the attic area to make sure there wasn't someone hiding in there. I became more and more paranoid that someone was in my house and I began having trouble sleeping. I felt like I was doing my best to soldier through at work and act as if I wasn't constantly worried about my home situation. However, I was anxious and felt like I wasn't doing enough.

It was the holiday season. I made several trips to Hobby Lobby and other places, spending frivolously on Christmas decorations. The shopping was to ease my mind, for some sort of reprieve from the recent chaos. During this time, I was dreaming big and journaling about those dreams, as well as the goals I wanted to accomplish. I was sure that these things would happen. For example, I just knew that I would be opening event venues in Austin, Houston, Kansas City and other cities, in old historic houses. That way, every time I would visit these cities, I would always have a place to stay. Although I still like the idea and it could happen one day, this was one of many ideas and some of them were far-fetched. I've always had big dreams and desires to do great things, but this was not the time.

Be a Life Breather

My life was unraveling before my eyes. I was going full speed ahead, in all directions and it was bound to come to a halt. I started to get sick. I had a cold and cough, a sore throat and was very sick for several weeks, but I did not make time to go to the doctor. Instead, I took an exorbitant amount of cough medicine, cough drops, decongestants, vitamin C and cold medicine. By this time, the work was completed on my house, but I still wasn't sleeping at all.

It all came to a head over a weekend when I hadn't slept. I was extremely paranoid, delirious, erratic, and not making sense. I felt completely at a loss. I didn't know what to do, so I called 911. I called my friend Angela right after. She knew what was going on and that I hadn't been sleeping and she told me to go to the hospital. At the time, I didn't know why I needed to go to the hospital, but I realized my mind wasn't in a good state, so I let the ambulance take me.

The doctor determined I had severe bronchitis. He said I didn't have any drugs in my system, but I had abnormally high levels of vitamin C from the pills I'd taken, as if that would make me all better. But the vitamin C levels weren't a concern for the doctor. After asking a bunch of questions, he explained what was happening. The doctor described it as a "textbook bipolar episode," meaning all of my symptoms were indicative of this preexisting disorder. This is when I learned I was bipolar. The ups and downs, the lows of depression and the highs of mania with the blind energy of racing thoughts, anxiety and paranoia, mood swings, erratic behavior, trouble sleeping, trouble concentrating, big ideas a.k.a. "grandiose thinking" and even big spending sprees, were all characterized as bipolar behavior.

I began seeing a psychiatrist and taking medications. I learned that I could have a full life, if I could manage the symptoms of bipolar disorder, take my medicine regularly and stay under the care of my psychiatrist. I was able to take some time off of work to get myself together. I took my medicine and met regularly with a therapist. I went back to work and tried to focus on that and getting well for a little while.

I had to try several different kinds of medication to find the right combination, which took a long time. Some medicines made me feel sick, one made my face break out, but mostly they made me really tired. They all mellowed me down, which I didn't like. I liked to be the fun, silly Chelsea, but the medicine often made me feel blah or complacent. We eventually found a combination that worked for me and I was on the lowest dosage of a couple different medications used to treat depression and bipolar disorder.

This was a particularly hard time in my life because I also felt like I was mourning my mom for the first time. I was back living in her neighborhood. I was shopping at the same grocery store. I was back in South Austin, but she was gone. And since my uncle totally ignored me even though he was still living in my mom's house, it felt like he was gone too. It was like I had no family in Austin because my uncle was reclusive and didn't keep in touch.

When I was 16 and my mom and Chris died, I had to grow up quickly. I had to get it together with all of the arrangements and finances. I was ahead of the game compared to my peers. I'd inherited my mom's house, gotten a new car, sold the house and bought my home in Houston. With Pam's help, I was investing in my retirement and writing off my mortgage interest, things that weren't even a concern to my peers. However, at some point during this time period, I fell behind my peers. My friends were getting good jobs, getting married, starting families and I was still partying, sparing no expense.

I continued working at the hotel downtown as their convention services coordinator for about a year and a half, still spending beyond my needs, still in party mode. I took my medicine as often as I remembered, but I always stayed up late, resulting in me being late to work. Eventually, in the fall of 2009, the hotel gave me an ultimatum: "Chelsea if you're late one more time, we will have to fire you." And guess what? I was late for the last time and I was fired. I realized, being a college graduate in a career that was perfect for me, I probably shouldn't be getting fired anymore. This was an eye opener.

KANSAS, THERE'S NO PLACE LIKE HOME

Initially, Pam suggested and I eventually agreed, that I should move to Kansas. I thought, maybe if I moved to Kansas to be closer to my family, I would have the support system I needed. I thought I could go for a bit, clean myself up and come back fresh to Austin. If nothing else, I could at least see what it was like to live near my family.

I wish I could say that my life got better, but it didn't. The next several years were a series of dead ends. I didn't know it at the time, but looking back, nothing panned out. As it turns out, I had less of a support system in Kansas. Pam was very busy with a full house. Although my family was only a couple hours away, I felt very alone because we didn't have a solid relationship and most of them did not come visit me. A few of them did, but I still felt let down. They had always said, "If only you lived closer, we could see you more often." I thought this move to Kansas was what I needed in order to have a closer relationship with my family. I expected to have a support system in Kansas, but it really wasn't there. I am not blaming them. I know that if I had communicated clearly and had proper expectations it probably would have been different. I just thought moving to Kansas was the solution and it didn't work out that way. My support system was still back in Austin where my friends and Mom and Chris's friends were.

The whole time I was in Kansas City, I tried to make friends, often going out by myself, attempting to spark friendships with people at bars. It didn't work out. People were different in Kansas. The people I met had grown up there and already had their cliques. It wasn't like Austin where people are more friendly, accepting, and often from other cities. As a result, I made a lot of the wrong kind of friends. Some of them were not positive influences in my life. A song comes to mind for this situation, from the movie *Urban Cowboy*, "Looking for love in all the wrong places." That describes it. There were a lot of takers. There were a lot of energy suckers. I tried not to judge others. I didn't feel like I was better than anyone else, so I tried my best to be supportive to many people with whom I probably should have cut ties.

Through all the ups and downs of my life, I can truthfully recognize that everything I did was to make things better. Even when I looked in the wrong places, I was still trying to improve my situation. I wasn't making the right choices, but at the time, I thought I was. When I show myself love now, I commend myself because I never stopped looking. Even with bad situation after bad situation, I never stayed and said, "Okay, this is good enough." I always continued to look for something better. There were failed friendships, failed jobs, abandoned jobs because I thought something else was better, failed relationships, and even a failed engagement. I had to go through all this to return to Austin and find that everything I was searching for was here all along. Here in Austin, my home.

I had moved to Kansas for a change, but it wasn't the change I was looking for. It wasn't until I returned to Austin, almost five years later, that things began to align and work out for the better. It's ironic to say that it wasn't a waste of time. I can imagine some person on the sidelines saying, "Okay, you needed a better support system, so you moved 800 miles away and knocked on 10,000 dead-end doors, then went back to where you started and found that your support system was there all along? What do you mean it's not a waste of time?!" But it wasn't. It had to happen, just the way it did. All of it was meant to happen in the exact and precise order that it did. Because if it hadn't, I wouldn't be sitting here now, years later, with a wonderful husband, two amazing step-kiddos who I love very much and a six-month-old sleeping baby boy in the next room, with whom I am totally infatuated.

From the experience, I learned that a geographical change did not change me because my problems came from within, so naturally they would follow. I also learned that change takes time. I couldn't rush it, although I tried. Also, I had always wanted to know what it was like to live near my family. I found that it was not best for me. I found my home and it was not in Kansas. And you know what? I also learned that I don't have to listen and operate my life based on what other people tell me. I have to follow my intuition. I must trust my gut. This lesson has slapped me upside the head so many times that you think I would have learned it sooner. But I didn't trust myself.

Be a Life Breather

There are so many lessons that could be taken from my life experiences in this chapter. Perhaps there is a lesson that will help with a problem you are experiencing. What is your struggle now? It may not be obvious or clear at this moment but it's something to think about. Is there something that is just not working, where it seems like you're trying to fit a square peg into a round hole? Maybe you are considering a change that can solve a problem for you or are weighing the pros and cons of a relationship or a business move. Would it be best to try something else, something new? Or possibly, is the answer right in front of you. Is there a different vantage point you could take that will change the view to reveal something you never saw before? Maybe someone else's perspective would be helpful. Maybe you simply need to reframe a situation or choose a different way to feel about it.

Whatever it is, you owe it to yourself to face your challenges head on. Do not make the mistake of running from your problems like I did. I assumed moving was going to make everything better and easier for me, but it didn't. Moving to Kansas made the situation ten times harder. Granted, I'm glad it happened because it all had to transpire to bring me where I am today, but this is a lesson that truly hits home. It's a lesson that I realize I must truly learn because I will be faced with it again.

Whatever lessons I learned, whatever lessons I didn't learn, I know now that it's all okay. We are who we are at this moment, and we are who we are meant to be. We can't blame ourselves for not being further along when we are on the right path. This is self-love. This is accepting our current reality knowing that we are going to continue to move forward. We must love ourselves enough to be okay with the mistakes we have made. I say it's better to make a mistake than to do nothing at all because at least we are doing something.

There are many concepts mentioned in this chapter, but it all boils down to this: we deserve to be loved. We are worthy of love. We are worthy of receiving love as well as giving love. Love yourself, you're all you've got. Be nicer to yourself. Give yourself a break sometimes. And realize that it's okay to make mistakes. Try to learn the lessons. If you don't, no worries, they will keep repeating until you've got them down. Remember that forgiveness goes hand-in-hand with love. Forgive yourself, love yourself and keep moving forward no matter what.

Ask yourself the following questions and consider your answers.

- Why am I my own worst critic?
- Why am I able to forgive others but not myself?
- How can I show love to my inner child?
- What would our future selves tell us now?
- How can I show myself more love now?

> **In the words of the wonderful *Lucille Ball,* "Love yourself first and everything else falls into line. You really have to love yourself to get anything done in this world."**

The Power of Self-Love Exercise

The exercise for this chapter has to do with self-forgiveness. The deeper you go, the freer you will become. What is it you judge most about yourself? What regrets do you have? Think back to some of the hardest times in your life. How do you feel about some of the decisions you made or the situations you got yourself into? How do those feelings affect you now?

_____

_____

_____

_____

SELF-FORGIVENESS LETTER

I was assigned a similar exercise by Elayna Fernandez earlier this year. I found it to be so transformational that I included a form of it here.

Write yourself a letter forgiving yourself for self-judgements, regrets, mistakes and ways that you feel you failed. Show yourself compassion and understanding. Reason with yourself and talk about the details surrounding that circumstance and how it ended up this way. Forgive yourself. Give yourself some grace. Allow yourself to move on.

_____

_____

_____

_____

_____

_____

_____

_____

_____

_____

_____

_____

_____

REFLECTION QUESTION

If you do not forgive yourself, and you carry shame for the shortcomings in your life, where will that lead you in five years?

CHAPTER 4

The Power of Purpose

You picked up this book for a reason. There is something more you want from life. If you are like most of us, we have big dreams that subside over time. We let the day in and day out define us because we've got to pay the bills and do the things, right? Many of us get caught in the hamster wheel of life and lose the fire that ignited the dreams inside of us in the first place. Many of us feel stuck because we are busy trying to make it and the thought of adding more to our plate seems impossible or unlikely to work out. Often, our time is consumed by the things we have to do in order to put food on the table for our family, keep the lights on, keep the home in order and stay afloat.

Think back for a moment and remember when you were a child and there was no doubt in your mind that you wanted your life to be different than the lives of some of the adults around you. I remember hearing adults and family members complain about the same things all the time and I just wondered, "Why don't you do something about it?" Yet I find myself making some of the same mistakes and repeating some of the same non-supportive patterns in my life.

Think for a moment:

- What did you want to do as a child?
- What kind of difference did you want to make?
- What kind of impact did you want to have?
- How did you see yourself showing up for your family?
- What are those "crazy dreams" in your heart?

- If money was no obstacle and you knew you could achieve anything in the world you wanted, what would you choose to do?

You see, we have those dreams inside us, but we tend to get stuck in the grind, thinking that at some point we will have time to do all the things we want to do.

"SOMEDAY ISLE"

In the teachings of Jim Rohn, he talks about, "Someday Isle." The idea is that we have so much on our plates that while juggling everything, we say to ourselves, "Someday I will…" fill in the blank. Hence, "Someday Isle." Someday, I will get organized. Someday, we will go to Hawaii. Someday, I will take the family to Disney World. Someday, I will go finish my degree. Unfortunately, that day often does not come.

Some of us daydream, but when we get back to "real life," we aren't taking the necessary steps to achieve those things we truly want. It is time for us to reap the benefits and happiness of achieving our dreams and all they entail. It is time to eliminate all time wasters and take steps toward our goals. As long as we have the right processes and steps, we can do this!

Let's elevate ourselves, which will elevate those around us. All we have to do to elevate, is love. It's simple. Love is the greatest form of energy. Let us love and live the life of our dreams and beyond, because we deserve it! We deserve better than right now! How do I know that? Because you're reading this book, which means you seek ways to improve yourself. Your growth is a priority and you enjoy learning how to become better. That's why you deserve it. Because you are doing your due diligence to keep moving forward and make progress. Rewards are already coming your way. Also, I know we deserve better because we have a dream in our hearts and it was put there for a reason. We have no idea what kind of ripple effects our actions will cause. The only person that is stopping you is you!

We must be dutiful to our dreams. We must give them all we've got, because we can make all the difference in the world, even if it is only one person. Imagine that through our dreams we can help many. There are struggling people that you have the ability to help. Aren't they worth it? Help others to avoid the pains you have experienced. Bless others. If you're blessed, be a blessing! Give your gifts! People just need to be noticed and cared for. People in your home and all around you need you to start loving them more right now.

Let's get off "Someday Isle" and get to a real island!

YOUR PURPOSE

Most of us at some point or another have tried to find our purpose in life, our "calling." Some people live their purpose every day. Some people have professions aligned with their purpose but have the desire to do more. Some people don't know their purpose at all. Other people know their purpose but are not sure how they are meant to execute it.

> **In the words of the iconic *Oprah Winfrey*, "There is no greater gift you can give or receive than to honor your calling. It's why you were born. And how you become most truly alive."**

Let's think about our purpose.

If you are not sure what your purpose is, take a guess at what it might be. If you have an idea of your life's purpose or what you were meant to do, are you doing it? How could you start implementing your purpose in your life right now?

Complete the following exercise regarding your purpose in life.

Purpose Exercise

What is your purpose?

_____
_____
_____
_____
_____
_____

How do you currently, or how could you, go about carrying out that purpose in your life?

_____
_____
_____
_____
_____
_____
_____

If you are having trouble with this exercise and are unclear on your purpose, ask yourself some of these questions:

- What fulfills you?
- What fills your cup?
- What makes you feel whole?
- What would it take to make your life feel complete?
- What do you want to help your family and others with?
- Everyone has a gift. What is your gift?
- If you're stuck, ask a trusted friend what they think your gift is.

You have something to offer the world. We were all innately designed to do something that no one else can do. You have a purpose. We all have a purpose. We are all unique and we were all designed in detail with care, love, and with our complete well-being and greatest potential in mind.

REFLECTION QUESTION

With your purpose in mind, why do you think you were chosen for this reason?

CHAPTER 5

The Power of Self-Awareness

By now, I hope you have started to dream again and that you have an idea of why you are here, your purpose. Now we can move forward. Just like in a shopping mall, we can look at the map to see where we want to go, but we must first know where we are. Only then can we figure out how to get where we want to go. We have to know the starting point and ending point to map out the correct path. In this chapter, we will get a good grasp on where we are at right now in our lives.

Wouldn't it be nice to define some of those inner fears and non-supportive patterns, so we could stop making the same mistakes? Allow us to figure out what to do and what not to do, in order to ensure our success and keep us on the right track.

> **In the words of the beautiful *Debbie Ford*, "Self-awareness is the ability to take an honest look at your life without any attachment to it being right or wrong, good or bad."**

THE PRESENT, A LOOK AT SELF

We have to take an honest look at ourselves, our strengths and weaknesses. We must be real with ourselves. For this chapter, we will zoom way out and look at the bird's-eye view of life. Imagine that you are looking down at your life as a whole. Can you see both where you want to be and where you are.

In order to be honest with yourself about where you are, you have to be the coach and the teammate. You will have to parent yourself. Think about this as if you were your future self. How would your future self, treat your younger self? Your goal in this chapter is to be the observer and the observed. You are the person doing the coaching and the person being coached.

Answer these questions to figure out where you are right now.

Greatest Accomplishments Exercise

What 5 things would you consider your greatest accomplishments?

1. _____

2. _____

3. _____

4. _____

5. _____

What do you love about your life?

_____
_____
_____
_____
_____
_____
_____

Chelsea Collie

What do you not love about your life?

___
___
___
___
___
___
___

What Needs to Change Exercise

Dig deep here. The more honest you are with yourself, the more you have to gain.

What's missing?

_____
_____
_____
_____

What needs to change now so that you can feel confident in moving forward to your goals and dreams?

_____
_____
_____
_____

This bird's-eye view is full circle. We know where we want to go. We know where we are now. Now, we must take a look at where we've been to determine the best path forward. Let us take a look back.

THE PAST

Think about your childhood. How were you brought up? What were your parents like? What did they believe? What did you believe? When you were a kid, what were your views on life? When you became a teenager, what were your views on life? What times were sad? What was the hardest? What did you learn? What did you learn not to do?

Because of what happened and the way you were treated, you learned some things that may or may not be true. We all learned a lot from our past, positive and negative. When we can identify the negative beliefs, we can prohibit them from stopping us in the future. We all have false beliefs from the past that hold us back, but we can choose a new reality. What are those false beliefs for you?

In a moment, you will be doing The Loving Truth Exercise. Here is an example of how I would complete this exercise.

THE LOVING TRUTH EXAMPLE:

I learned at age 16, when my mom died, that sooner or later, everyone leaves. She was my closest and #1 person on earth, and suddenly she was gone.

Also, I had very high achievers and high producers around me, so I often felt inadequate. I have struggled with not feeling good enough and feeling like I'm not doing enough, not cutting it. That's the bad part.

Now, here's the good part. We get to replace false beliefs with the truth, the loving truth that we would tell a friend. What I have realized through having an amazing, supportive husband, is that not everyone leaves. So that is the truth I use to replace my false belief.

Be a Life Breather

For my feelings of inadequacy, I conclude that I have always done my best with the tools I had at that particular time. Sometimes it was all I could do to get out of bed, and that was enough. It was enough because I survived, I'm still going and I will never give up.

Here's how I would complete this exercise:

False Belief	The Loving Truth
Everyone leaves	Not everyone leaves, some people stay
I'm not good enough	I have always done my best, with the tools I had at that particular time.

The Loving Truth Exercise

Now it's your turn. Identify 5 false beliefs and correct them with the loving truth.

5 False Beliefs	The Loving Truth

Give yourself some kudos for being honest and standing in your truth. You deserve a good life. Not only do you deserve grace, you deserve to give yourself that grace.

As we learned in Chapter 3: The Power of Self-Love, we cannot give what we do not have. We must love ourselves first because we have to help ourselves before we can help others. Rise up. Step into your greatness. It's your time. You deserve it. You deserve better. Those hopes and dreams were put inside of you for a reason. You were meant to achieve them. You were meant for more.

Now, pay attention to your thoughts. What reactive thoughts have you had so far? For example, if you said in your head, "Yeah right, I can't do this," put that on your false belief list. Replace it with the truth, something like, "This is easy. I can do this." Let's begin thinking empowering thoughts.

TOOL

From now on, be an observer of your thoughts. Pay attention to what those thoughts are telling you. Do this for the next few days. Pretend as if you are a scientist conducting an experiment. When negative thoughts pop up, DRM them, which means: Delete. Replace. Move. In practice, this means that when a negative thought appears, you recognize it, reject it, and then replace it with the truth and carry on.

Put this tool in your toolbox and use it to identify and reduce your negative thoughts.

D – Delete
R – Replace with truth
M – Move (carry on)

Acknowledge the false thoughts and recognize that they are non-supportive. Replace it or correct it and continue on with your day. The more you do it, the more natural it will become.

TWO HELPFUL TIPS:

- I find it helpful to take my right pointer finger and touch my palm at the center of my left hand. It's a physical motion. The thought moves into an action. As you press your right finger into the palm of your left hand, say in your head, "delete." Then replace with the truth and continue.

- You can also wear a rubber band around your wrist. Or for girls you can wear a ponytail holder on your wrist. When those thoughts come up, pop the rubber band. Popping the rubber band is your "delete." Replace the thought with the truth. Then move and continue with your day.

When you "move," you take action on the next right thing. Here's where your focus, your priorities, and your daily tasks come in. You will know what you need to do. Soon, we will have determined what steps we are taking each day. We simply redirect our focus and take that next right step.

Staying on track is an extremely hard thing to do, but it is a simple process. As we continue to work on this, it gets easier and quicker. Soon enough we begin gaining time because we're not letting our fears slow us down. We are procrastinating less. Soon we are making traction. Very soon we are moving closer to our goals every day. Everyone has fears. But only some of us have the tools to prevent those fears from hindering us. Are we going to use them?

> "Go where you are celebrated – not tolerated. If they can't see your true value and worth, then it's time for a new start." – *Author unknown*

CUT THE CRAP

We get what we tolerate. Once we start standing up for ourselves, we will stop letting others stomp all over us. Vow not to tolerate any more crap. If someone belittles you, you do not have to take it. You do not have to listen to it. In fact, it's only hindering you if you do. By allowing others to treat you less than, you are disrespecting yourself and you're sending the wrong message, leading others to believe it's okay to disrespect you.

Part of showing up for yourself is having your own back, standing up for yourself when others don't and even walking away when someone doesn't seem to be getting the message. Often, we put up with situations to avoid conflict and "keep the peace." Some battles aren't worth fighting, however, many are still happening because we have yet to put our foot down.

When we want to get better, we do not simply add a bunch of things to our plate. We eliminate what is not serving us. If something is sucking the life out of you, cut it off! You can eliminate it, you can change the way you go about dealing with it, or you can change your attitude about it so that it's no longer painful for you.

Not too long ago, there were two business-related issues in my life that were really keeping me awake at night. They were heavy on my heart, and quite frankly, it sucked. When I totally ended it with both of those things, I had a freedom I hadn't felt in a long time. If it's not a good feeling, it's bringing you down, or it's not worth the trouble it's causing you, then eliminate it. We can call it prioritizing.

What gives you anxiety? What keeps you up at night? What are you putting up with that you are no longer willing to tolerate? What can you eliminate from your life to reduce stress? What or who wears you out? Who and what drains you? What are you tired of? What things are taking your time and not paying off?

Purging Exercise

Commit to removing two things off your plate. If you can't totally quit it, decide how you can change the situation so it is less stressful for you. What two things can you eliminate or change in order to reduce stress and keep moving forward?

1. _____

2. _____

One last lesson from the past: When you start to improve, do better, and start making some traction, is there something you sometimes do that derails you or gets you off track? In what ways have you sabotaged yourself? What are the mistakes you keep making that keep you stuck and not moving forward?

List three behaviors that derail you from your progress?

3 Red Flags – What Not to Do

1. _____

2. _____

2. _____

When these non-supportive behaviors or beliefs come up in your life, recognize them as red flags. Vow not to keep making the same mistakes. Tell yourself to keep moving forward and go.

We don't have to be stuck in the past. Life is like a windshield. Your past is in the rearview mirror. We can't go forward when we're looking back. Let us accept the mistakes of the past and give ourselves permission to live our best future. When you show up for yourself, really show up! Stand tall. Strike a power pose. Put your hands on your hips or do as I do and put your hand on your heart. Feel the energy; multiply the energy around you. Tell yourself the truth about who you are. The truth is that you are doing your best. You are a good person. You don't quit.

MANTRA – A STATEMENT OR SLOGAN REPEATED FREQUENTLY

Your Mantra

Give yourself an affirmative thought. For example, "I am strong" or "I am worthy." This statement is what makes you feel powerful. Use what sounds right for you.

My personal mantra is: "I am strong. I can achieve anything I set my mind to." When I get down or feel stuck, I remind myself I can achieve anything.

What is your mantra?

_____

_____

Throughout the day, when those false beliefs pop up, correct them and continue. Delete Replace and Move. Replace it with your mantra if you want. As often as you can remember throughout the day, say your mantra to yourself. Think it and say it! Say your mantra verbally, whenever possible, and with passion and conviction. The more real you make it, the more real it becomes.

> **In the words of the intelligent *Brendon Burchard,* "I'm not interested in your limiting beliefs, I'm interested in what makes you limitless."**

ACTION ITEMS CHALLENGE:
- When those non-supportive thoughts come up, recognize them as a red flag. Delete, Replace and Move forward.
- Make a commitment that you will say your mantra as often as you can.

LET'S RECAP! NOW WE:
- Know our purpose
- Know what's been stopping us and have tools to overcome those non-supportive thoughts and actions.
- Know the red flags to look out for so we do not self-sabotage and stay consistently on the path to success
- Have a mantra to help us focus and keep moving forward

Next up, vision! Let's paint a picture of our greatest life.

REFLECTION QUESTION

If we were able to eliminate our biggest challenge right now, what could we do as a result?"

CHAPTER 6

The Power of Vision

It's very important that we keep our dreams alive or reignite that spark inside of us if we have neglected it. As we know, we have a purpose and our dreams exist for a reason. In our greatest potential we are meant to achieve them. It's time to "place your order with the universe." Let's DREAM BIG and get some of our heart's desires down on paper. What are your crazy dreams? What items are on your bucket list of the things you want to do before you die?

Here are some questions to ponder:

- What would you like some of your greatest life achievements to be?
- What are some experiences you would love to be able to share with your family and friends? What monumental tasks could help you to achieve your purpose and your greatest potential?
- Where would you like to travel?
- Where would you like to live?
- What would you like to drive?
- Do you want to have a vacation home? Or several?!
- How much money would you love to have in your savings account, your emergency fund, your retirement account, or invested?
- What would be a super successful amount of income you would like to achieve in a given year? How do you want to help others?
- How would you like to give?

Be a Life Breather

- What difference do you want to make?
- What impact do you want to have?

It is possible. It is possible FOR YOU to achieve and receive the desires of your heart. You must believe it is possible. You must love yourself enough to allow these dreams to come into fruition. You must have faith that if you take the necessary actions, these things will show up.

Do not hold back. If you were living your purpose, what could you accomplish? Do not pre-judge. Accept that there are no limitations. Accept that money s no object.

If you could do anything, if you knew you couldn't fail, what would you do?

Bucket List Exercise

Write down a minimum of 25 do-before-you-die items.

Remember, anything is possible. Dream big!

1. _____
2. _____
3. _____
4. _____
5. _____
6. _____
7. _____
8. _____
9. _____
10. _____
11. _____
12. _____
13. _____
14. _____
15. _____

Be a Life Breather

16. _____
17. _____
18. _____
19. _____
20. _____
21. _____
22. _____
23. _____
24. _____
25. _____

BONUS: Add a few more, why not?!

26. _____
27. _____
28. _____
29. _____
30. _____

Did you complete your bucket list? This step is crucial to achieve your highest potential.

Give yourself a pat on the back! Many people do not allow themselves to dream or do not consider their dreams anymore. They have let them go. Most do not put them down on paper. However, you are different. You want better. You want more. You know there is a better, brighter future out there for you and your loved ones. Some people who have accomplished many of their dreams are now living beyond them. Imagine you are one of those people. Look at your list and imagine that some of these items are small stepping stones to even greater realizations in your life.

Take a few moments to imagine what it would feel like to have checked all of these dreams and goals off your list. Imagine that all these things and even more have happened in your life.

You will have these things. You will accomplish these goals. If you are dutiful to your dreams, you will achieve them or better. Of course, not everything will work out exactly as we plan, but remember: this or something better. When doors close or when things don't work out, try to keep in mind that there is something even better, already on its way to you.

This step is crucial in order to prepare yourself for mapping out a plan. This is the point where we paint a picture of who we will become. Look far out, 20 years or more, and imagine what kind of person you have grown into. Consider that you have achieved all of the items on your bucket list, or better. Write in as much detail as possible about your BIG vision. Write about your family, where you live, your daily life, your houses/cars, the state of your career or business(es). Write down everything that is important for you to achieve in your lifetime.

You have achieved your greatest dreams, you have accomplished your goals and you have become an incredible person in the process. Write in past tense as if you have already accomplished all your goals and dreams. Be grateful that you have received these things.

Who have you become? In the next 20 years and beyond, who are you?

The BIG Vision Exercise

Fill in the blank:

I have achieved my highest potential. I am so happy and grateful now that:

_____
_____
_____
_____
_____
_____
_____
_____
_____
_____
_____
_____
_____
_____
_____
_____

Great, now we break it down. We have our BIG vision, 20 years or more. We are simply going to break it down: 20 years, 10 years, 5 years, 2 years, 1 year. Break it down into parts. Use numbers wherever possible to break down more easily.

For Example:
One part of my big vision is to have 100 rental properties. So I broke the numbers down. In 10 years, I want to have 50 rentals. In 5 years, I want to have 25 rentals. In 2 years, I want to have 10 rentals. In 1 year, I want to have 5 rental properties.

First, let's write the dates so we can have a better idea as we are planning.

Today's Date: _____

Date in 1 year: _____

Date in 2 years: _____

Date in 5 years: _____

Date in 10 years: _____

Date in 20 years: _____

Again, write in past-tense. List all the things you have become. List all the things you have achieved.

What do you need to achieve in 10 years to be on the right track to achieving that BIG vision?

10-Year Vision:
I am so happy and grateful now that:

_____

_____

_____

_____

What do you need to achieve in 5 years to be on the right track to achieving that 10-year vision?

5-Year Vision:
I am so happy and grateful now that:

_____

_____

_____

_____

What do you need to achieve in two years to be on the right track to achieve that five-year vision?

2-Year Vision:
I am so happy and grateful now that:

_____

_____

_____

_____

What do you need to achieve in one year to be on the right track to achieve that 2-year vision?

1-Year Vision:
I am so happy and grateful now that:

_____

_____

_____

_____

Congrats! Take a moment to celebrate your accomplishments. You have a vision. You know where you want to go. You know where you need to be in one year to be on the right track. Most people do not take the time to dream, set goals, and put them on paper. You are ahead of most!

> **In the words of the legendary *Steve Jobs*, "If you are working on something exciting that you really care about, you don't have to be pushed. The vision pulls you."**

Now what? Time to hammer out our plan! It's time to put the pen to the paper and map out how we get to our goals. You can do this.

REFLECTION QUESTION

What do we see if we have no vision?

CHAPTER 7

The Power of Strategy

You have now arrived at one of the most important steps, the plan. The plan we will create in this chapter is the strategy we need to achieve our big dreams and reach our highest potential. If you fail to plan, you plan to fail. The key is to make it clear and simple.

You will learn the easiest way to break down your 1-year vision into small bite-sized daily, weekly, and 12-week chunks. Allow me to explain the process so you can get the most out of this chapter and complete the exercises necessary to map out the next year.

In the process of writing this book, I came across a book that I love called *The 12 Week Year* by Brian P. Moran and Michael Lennington. It coincides perfectly with what I am teaching. I highly recommend you pick up the book. It's particularly useful regarding mapping out goals and plans. *The 12 Week Year* goes into great detail in regard to the planning process as well as the foundations of why this system works.

I am paraphrasing here, but basically the book argues that one can achieve in 12 weeks, what they would normally achieve in one year. Because of the longer time frame of one year, there are more variables. Therefore, you have more control over the variables in a shorter time frame. If you concisely define your goals and break them down into detailed steps, the same amount of progress can be achieved in a quarter of the time.

There are 52 weeks in a year, and 52 divided by 4 is 13. There are 4 equal 13-week sections in one year. Therefore, *The 12 Week Year* recommends that you plan in 12-week segments. Week 13 is a time to celebrate your successes, analyze what you have accomplished, and define the plan for the next 12 weeks.

Brian P. Moran, Michael Lennington, and their team have had thousands of people go through this process and they have fine-tuned the system into one that works. The authors explain it better than I ever could. I recommend you buy the book and the accompanying workbook, *The 12 Week Year Field Guide* to further solidify your plan. You can have access to sample plans and tools as well as purchase the book at https://12weekyear.com/.

In looking at the 1-year vision you defined in Chapter 6, you will need to prioritize the five most important items you need to accomplish by the end of year one, to be on the right track to your 2-year vision. Take a look and define those goals now.

1-Year Goals:
What are the 5 most important items you need to accomplish by the end of year 1, in order to be on the right track to your 2-year vision?

Define your major 1-year goals here.

1. _____

2. _____

3. _____

4. _____

5. _____

Looking at these goals, decide which goal needs to be achieved first. Number the goals 1–5 in order of importance. Now it's time to get a game plan for the first 12 weeks.

In order to be on track with your 1-year goals, what 3 goals do you need to accomplish in the next 12 weeks?

12-Week Goals:

1. _____

2. _____

3. _____

Now you will break down each 12-week goal into the steps to get there. Include the deadlines, whenever possible, for when each step or task should be completed.

Complete the plan for each 12-week goal:

Goal # 1:_____
Steps to get there:

_____

_____

_____

Goal # 2:_____
Steps to get there:

_____

_____

_____

Goal # 3:_____
Steps to get there:

_____

_____

_____

You are so close to being on your way! Let's close it out and get started living our best life!

> **In the words of the enlightening *Lee Bolman*, "A vision without a strategy remains an illusion."**

REFLECTION QUESTION

What would it mean to you if you could fully count on yourself and know that if you commit to something, it will be done?

CHAPTER 8

The Power of Execution

Ideas, knowledge, and intentions are all just thoughts until executed. All the planning in the world won't get you anywhere unless you take action. But first, remember that it is okay to seek help. Sometimes in our lives, we are so caught up in our circumstances that we can't see a way out. That's when we need to call a friend or family member, or call on a professional. I, myself, have had a therapist for years, and that has made a very positive impact on my life. Most likely, you have certain people you count on for help in certain areas of your life. It's important you are clear on who your support system is. For example, who do you reach out to when it comes to getting your feelings hurt, getting your finances together, or when you're upset?

Support System Exercise

Name 3–5 people you can call on for help. Define what they can help you with:

_____

_____

_____

_____

_____

For moments of weakness, if all else fails, who can you call?

_____

Since you are taking the necessary steps to improve your life, it's not a bad idea to call up these people and tell them about your plans and goals. Go ahead and ask them if you can count on their support, if and when you need it. Also, find someone who is a positive influence and has similar goals to have an excellent accountability partner. Do whatever you can to set yourself up for success. It's time to kick it into high gear. Remember, others are waiting for your gifts!

GO TIME!

Now that we know we have what it takes, we believe in ourselves, and we use our mantra to carry on when life gets tough, it's time to take action and become that person we know we can be. All the planning in the world won't get us anywhere unless we take action.

It's time to get out the calendar. Let's make this happen! Your calendar will be essential to your success. Use a calendar you are comfortable with, whether it be physical or digital. Be sure to have it with you at all times and keep it updated with your goals. Be sure your calendar has monthly and weekly views.

To begin, you will need to decide on your start date. You can choose to go along with the four quarters of a year, but the system is designed around (4) 13-week periods, so you can decide which week you would like to start. It's up to you if you want to start this week, next week, or at the beginning of next month, etc. I recommend you start on a Monday.

So, you have your calendar. What is your start date? _____

In your calendar, go ahead and number the weeks, 1–13, 1–13, 1–13, 1–13, all the way through one year from your start date.

Write the dates of the 12th and 13th weeks of the four timeframes here:

First 12 weeks

Start Date (beginning of 12 weeks) _____

End Date (end of 12 weeks) _____

13th week (start and end date) _____

Second 12 weeks

Start Date (beginning of 12 weeks) _____

End Date (end of 12 weeks) _____

13th week (start and end date) _____

Third 12 weeks

Start Date (beginning of 12 weeks) _____

End Date (end of 12 weeks) _____

13th week (start and end date) _____

Fourth 12 weeks

Start Date (beginning of 12 weeks) _____

End Date (end of 12 weeks) _____

13th week (start and end date) _____

Now record in your calendar:

- Your 3 main goals for the first 12 weeks
- Your steps or tasks to achieving those goals and the corresponding due dates

BIG ROCKS AND LITTLE ROCKS

For my personal planner, I use the Franklin Covey classic-sized planner. I love it. They have several choices of designs to choose from as far as the paper, and they have beautiful binders that can fit your personal style. If you are looking for a new planner and would like to see what they have available, you can go to: https://shop.franklinplanner.com/.

Be a Life Breather

Several years ago, I attended a Franklin Covey time management course where I learned a wealth of good information for defining, planning, and prioritizing properly. The course teaches value-based planning where you first define your values and roles you play in life, and you build your goals, priorities, and tasks based on those deep-rooted values. One of the main things I remember from that course was the lesson of the big rocks and little rocks, and I want to share that with you.

At the event, the speaker told a story. The speaker described a time when there were two men, a large glass jar, a bowl of big rocks, and a bowl of small rocks. For clarity's sake, we will name the two men Fred and Bob. Fred asked Bob to fit all the rocks into the glass jar. Accepting the challenge, Bob proceeded to pour the small rocks into the jar. Then Bob proceeded to put the large rocks into the jar, one by one. Bob filled the glass jar, but he still had many of the big rocks left. All the rocks did not fit. Bob looked puzzled and looked to Fred.

Fred took all the big and small rocks out of the jar and put them back in their respective bowls. He said, "Now, watch this." Fred placed all of the large rocks in the glass jar. Then he poured some of the small rocks and shook up the jar until the small rocks fell down in between the cracks of the big rocks. Some of the small rocks trickled down to the bottom of the glass jar. Then he poured some more small rocks and shook the jar to allow the small rocks to fall again. He continued to do this until all the rocks, big and small, were in the jar. All the rocks fit.

At Franklin Covey time management seminars, they tell this story to illustrate that we all have important things that need to be done each week. Some of these important tasks are things we need to complete every week, and some do not need to be completed on a regular basis.

Your "musts"—tasks that have to be done—are your big rocks. It's important to schedule those big rocks in, whenever possible, prior to the start of each week. Once you schedule those big rocks, you can then schedule your appointments and your tasks—your little rocks—in between. That is the key to fitting all your tasks in and ensuring that you have allocated enough time during the week to address your priorities.

KEEP SCORE

The 12 Week Year suggests keeping score. Keeping score helps you track how many tasks you complete on a given day. The daily score is referred to as an "execution rate." Keeping score is a great, easy way to hold yourself accountable. I recommend you keep score on a regular basis.

You may choose to keep score five, six, or seven days a week. Decide on a reasonable number of items to complete on a daily basis. Would you like to focus on completing two things per day or ten things per day? I find three to five tasks to be ideal. The number will change with your schedule. For example, maybe you have a family gathering on Thursday, so you choose to complete five things on Wednesday and two things on Thursday. No matter how many tasks you have on a given day, I have found that percentages work best when recording your execution rate. For example, if you planned to complete ten things in a day and you completed nine, that's a score of 90 percent for the day. If you planned to complete five things and you completed three, that's 60 percent.

Even if you have not completed as much as you would have liked, continue to keep score because that is what is going to make you better over time. According to Moran and Lennington, you have a good chance of completing your 12-week goals if you can hit an 85 percent or better execution rate on average per week. Even if you hit 60 or 70 percent, you're still ahead of where you were before beginning this process.

WEEKLY

Your weekly and daily plans are the keys to your success. Since the week is usually pretty full and Saturdays are often busy, Sunday is the best day to prepare for a productive week.

On "set-up-your-week Sundays," you will total and average your execution scores for the previous week. You should write everything down for the coming week in your calendar. Identify your big rocks and little rocks. Record your appointments and goals, and allot time for your priorities by scheduling them in your calendar.

Every Sunday, look at your monthly view and make sure all your appointments and social engagements are also written in the weekly section of your calendar. For people using paper planners, it is an important step to have all your appointments in the monthly and weekly sections. The weekly section will be your more detailed working calendar because it looks at the week as a whole and provides more space than the monthly view. .

Think about your family and what their needs are from you, such as movie nights or date nights, and be sure to schedule that in. Do you have any upcoming events in your e-mail that should be in your calendar? Also, perhaps you RSVP'd to an event on social media. Put that on your calendar as well. Get it all in there.

Review the deadlines you have for the coming week and make sure those are noted on the weekly view of your calendar. Determine any steps that need to be completed prior to those due dates so you are prepared to meet your deadlines and schedule those in. Also, double check that you are on track with your overall 12-week goals and deadlines. If you have specific goals for the week, make sure those are scheduled on the specific days as well.

Time block whenever possible. Making the space and setting those timeframes ahead of time will set you up for success, especially when it comes to your priorities, as it will help you organize and plan each day. Remember, things are bound to change, but we do our best to set ourselves up for success and allow ourselves to be flexible when things change. This is also a good time to compare your average execution rate to previous weeks and see how well you are executing your goals.

Now for the daily.

DAILY

The best planning for the next day starts the night before. Prior to the end of each day, define your priorities for the next day. This ensures that when you wake up, you have your priorities and commitments already laid out. If you can't plan the night before, determine those tasks or goals prior to starting your work for the day.

Throughout the day, continue to check things off your list, delegate tasks, or reschedule to another day. Alarms are great reminders to get started at a specific time, especially when it comes to phone calls, webinars, video calls, or leaving for an important meeting.

Each evening or at the end of the workday, check to see what tasks you have completed and what tasks are still outstanding. If you set out to complete five tasks and you completed four, score yourself an 80 percent for your execution rate and move the uncompleted task to the next day, another day on your calendar, or delete.

13TH WEEK

Remember, if you stay on track and focused, you can accomplish in 12 weeks what it takes others a year or longer to accomplish. On the 13th week after each 12-week period, you will celebrate your milestones, reflect on the last 12 weeks, and set your goals and intentions for the next 12 weeks.

When you celebrate milestones, treat yourself in some way as a reward for a job well done. This is something for you and you alone. Buy yourself something you have been wanting, take a book to the park—reward yourself in a way that's right for you. It's great to take out your spouse or loved ones and have a celebratory dinner, but be sure to do something special just for yourself. When you take this time for yourself, stay in that place of gratitude for the progress you have made. Soak it all in and be proud of yourself. You had dreams, goals, and a vision, and you made it happen.

I recommend journaling so you can see how you improve with each 12-week period. During this time, you will review what you have completed and what you were unable to complete. Look over your weekly averaged execution rates. Think about and identify what worked and what didn't. Conclude what might work better next time. Sit down and determine your three goals for the next 12 weeks. Write out all the steps you can think of that will help you achieve each goal and assign due dates. Record the goals and steps in your calendar with the corresponding due dates.

You will find that with each 12-week period, you are able to make more and more traction on the path to your greatest goals and dreams. The longer you do this, the easier it will become and the quicker you will excel.

MOMENTUM

Once you have your vision and your strategy, and you've been executing your strategy, the people you need most start coming to you. That's how you really know you are on the right track. You will start meeting people randomly who are the exact person you need at that moment. Also, you will learn more about people you already know, finding that they have similar goals and dreams. Life gives us what we need; we simply must recognize it when it happens.

The law of attraction plays a huge part here. What you track grows. What you focus on expands. Once you write down your goals and dreams—specifically your 12-week goals and dreams and steps to get there—the universe will start aligning everything to deliver that to you. You will see things you didn't see before. Because you are focusing and taking action, these things will find you.

Execution Exercise

Refer back to pages 80 & 81 to review your 12 week goal.

Based on your 12 week goal, what is your 1 month goal? (1-3 maximum, less is more)

_____

Based on your 1 month goal, what are your weekly priorities for this week? What are your "big rocks?" What are your "little rocks?" Identify and be sure to schedule these in your calendar.

_____

_____

_____

_____

What tasks do you need to complete tomorrow? Identify and schedule these in your calendar.

Get started!

- Do your best to complete these tasks tomorrow. Cross things off as you complete them.
- At the end of the day tomorrow, specify what was completed and not completed. Calculate your execution rate (percentage) and record your score in your calendar.
- Repeat!

REFLECTION QUESTION

How would it feel to look back at the last four weeks and see that you averaged a 90 percent execution rate?

Conclusion

Remember what you learned:

- You always have a choice, no matter what. By not making a choice, you have still made a choice. If there is something you are not okay with, you can do something about it and/or choose to look at the situation from a better, more empowering angle.

- Remember, love conquers all. Love can help any situation. Love can change everything. In order to create more love in the world, we simply must start with those around us.

- Love yourself. We cannot give what we don't have. We can only help others to the extent that we have helped ourselves. In order to make a bigger impact we must love ourselves and elevate ourselves to an even higher place.

- Keep your vision fresh. Revisit it as often as you can in your mind. Daydream, expand, and elaborate on all the details of the life that will be yours. Think of the impact you were meant to make, your purpose. You are here for a greater reason than we know. We were all meant for more, more than what we are now.

- Remember the power of self-awareness and being honest with ourselves. It is okay that we are not perfect. But we must admit our faults and work to improve them for our loved ones. It is essential that we have our own backs. We must stand up for ourselves. Remember your mantra and repeat it to yourself. Remember DRM: Delete, Replace, and Move. Delete those negative thoughts and unsupportive beliefs. Replace them with the loving truth, and no matter what, keep moving forward.

- Have a plan. If we have our strategy in place, we will make progress towards our goals and dreams. We can always course correct on the way. Remember your long-term vision, your 1-year vision, and your 12-week goals.

- Execution is key. Our strategy is inconsequential unless we put our plan into action. With the right attitude, tools, and accountability we will have the support we need in order to accomplish the steps toward achieving our goals.
- Spread love and speak life into one another with every chance you get.
- Be a life breather. Elevate yourself to elevate those around you.

I leave you with my favorite quote.

> **In the words of the amazing visionary, *Walt Disney*, "Around here, however, we don't look backwards for very long. We keep moving forward, opening up new doors and doing new things, because we're curious ... and curiosity keeps leading us down new paths."**

It's been an honor to share this information with you. Thank you for reading. Remember you are worth showing up for. You can achieve anything you set your mind to. You deserve an even fuller life. You are worth it. Keep moving forward, and may we never be the same.

Resources You Can Tap Into

There are multiple ways to get involved with our Spread Love Speak Life Movement. If you would like more information, go to spreadlovespeaklife.com and submit your e-mail address for a wealth of free content, and to find out about the various ways we can support you as an individual, business, entrepreneur, and fellow life breather.

After speaking with some amazing people, I have found that many of them are already trying to bring more love into the world in their specific markets and businesses. And like me, they wanted a community in which members could encourage one another and let others know they are not alone.

Now, our goal is to have an online platform where we can highlight individuals and businesses who are showing love in their own communities. If you have an idea or a business, this platform will be a valuable benefit for you. Remember, for organizations to be great they must be of service to everyone. Together we can do more. When more than one person asks for the same thing, it will be given. Imagine all the good we can do together.

At spreadlovespeaklife.com, we look at the big picture, zooming way out to help you see your life as a whole, to take stock and complete an accurate assessment of where you are today. We help you to identify those true desires, the dreams you knew you would achieve when you were a child. Start dreaming again in your everyday life! Take those desires and that destination you want to reach and put an action plan to it. You can and will achieve definiteness of purpose.
We want to spread more love together, speak more life into others and create an even better life for those on board with the Spread Love Speak Life Movement.

To get connected:

- Follow us on Facebook, Instagram, and Twitter at Be a Life Breather
- Join our Spread Love Speak Life Community group on Facebook to be further supported in our network and find out how you can benefit personally and professionally
- Text "BUCKETLIST" to 26786 to claim your complimentary Bucket List Blueprint

We look forward to staying connected to you. Thank you for the love. Know that you are loved. Know that love can change anything and everything. We wish you the absolute best.

FREE GIFT!

As a thank you for purchasing this book, the author has granted you a complimentary tool, the **Bucket List Blueprint**.

The most important first step to defining your dreams and goals is to complete your bucket list. In addition to the book, the Bucket List Blueprint is a supplemental tool which will assist you when completing your bucket list.

How do you get it?

Text "BUCKETLIST" TO 26786 to claim your free Bucket List Blueprint

The Bucket List Blueprint contains three elements:
1. Video: Bucket List Overview
2. Audio: Powerful Future-Self Visualization Exercise
3. Bucket List PDF

In the "Bucket List Blueprint," you will be welcomed with a video explaining how the Bucket List Blueprint works.

Next, you will listen to a short but powerful 15-minute Audio Visualization where you will travel forward in time to meet your future self, which will enable you to better see what dreams and goals you were destined to experience.

Finally, you will come out of the visualization exercise and make your bucket list with the PDF provided. Best wishes moving forward!

Statue of Responsibility

A portion of the proceeds of each book sold will support this incredible cause.

The Statue of Responsibility is the vision of Dr. Viktor E. Frankl, holocaust survivor, and author of *Man's Search for Meaning*. In his book, Frankl states that for America to maintain her freedoms, she must "bookend" her Statue of Liberty on the East Coast with a Statue of Responsibility on the West Coast. World-renowned sculptor, Gary Lee Price has been commissioned to do just that.

Join us n this history-making endeavor.

It's more than a Monument, it's a Movement!

**For more information, visit:
www.statueofresponsibility.com**

Top 50+ most influential people to watch and learn from:

- Oprah
- Sharon Lechter
- Tony Robbins
- Kim Kardashian
- Mel Robbins
- Angel Tuccy
- Danelle Delgado
- Phyllis Newhouse
- Bill Walsh
- Susie Carder
- John Maxwell
- Dani Johnson
- Bob Proctor
- Sonia Ricotti
- Joe Dispenza
- Forbes Riley
- Les Brown
- Rita Davenport
- Eiji Morishita
- Elayna Fernandez
- Beverly Zeimet
- Michelle Jewsbury
- Ken Rochon
- Carey Conley
- Michelle Faust
- Zondra Evans
- Leesa Clark-Price & Gary Lee Price
- Tim Ballard
- Lisa Nichols
- Kelly Clarkson
- Michael Beckwith
- Sara Bazan
- Leah Remini
- Christine McKay
- Jen Fontanilla
- Kris Jenner
- Jack Canfield
- Marianne Williamson
- Tina Torres
- LaChelle Adkins
- Rhonda Byrnes
- Robert Carlisle
- John Assaraf

Be a Life Breather

- Melanie McSally
- Kate Northrup
- Merri-jo Hillaker
- Suze Orman
- Lori Tisinai
- Michelle Obama
- Madonna
- Sheila Alexander
- Ellen
- Abraham Hicks
- Grandma Sparky
- Reverend Kevin Lee
- Jada Pinkett Smith
- Will Smith
- Kylie Jenner
- Monica Mojica
- Patti Grover
- Jill Reynolds
- Demi Moore
- Robert Collier
- Jeanetta Collier
- Matthew McConaughey
- Emmanuel Acho
- Lady Gaga
- Lisa Copeland

About the Author

Chelsea Collie is the CEO of Spread Love Speak Life whose vision is to elevate the world by the power of love. Chelsea has an entrepreneurial spirit, which opens the door to inspire and serve others through her community. Her mission is to empower 10,000 moms to achieve their one big dream by 2030.

Having had a traumatic experience at the age of 16, she found herself without a mother. Chelsea had the option of letting loss and heartbreak rule her destiny or finding the power to rise above. She chose to let her experience propel her forward in her mission of helping others.

Chelsea currently resides in Austin, Texas, with her husband, children, and pets. She and her husband enjoy investing in real estate and renovating properties. Chelsea's hobbies include live music, attending personal growth events, and spending time with friends.

She has become unstoppable and so can you.

Learn more at www.spreadlovespeaklife.com

CREATING DISTINCTIVE BOOKS
WITH INTENTIONAL RESULTS

We're a collaborative group of creative masterminds with a mission to produce high-quality books to position you for monumental success in the marketplace.

Our professional team of writers, editors, designers, and marketing strategists work closely together to ensure that every detail of your book is a clear representation of the message in your writing.

Want to know more?
Write to us at info@publishyourgift.com
or call (888) 949-6228

Discover great books, exclusive offers, and more at
www.PublishYourGift.com

Connect with us on social media

@publishyourgift

www.ingramcontent.com/pod-product-compliance
Lightning Source LLC
Chambersburg PA
CBHW042026100526
44587CB00029B/4309